THE MAGNIFICENT
BRITISH GARDEN ROBIN

IN HIS OWN WORDS

A valuable source of practical information
concerning Britain's favourite bird

By A. ROBIN, Esq.

To Mrs Robin

ISBN: 9798483526490

en–gb used throughout

CONTENTS

List of Illustrations

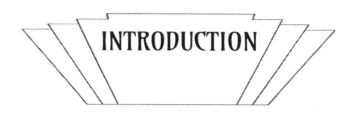

INTRODUCTION

Now, I expect you're reading this because you already like robins. That's a good start. Because although it's true that robins can be a bit on the cheeky side and full of themselves, it's also a well–known fact that you can't be in a garden when a robin is singing and not feel just a little bit happy at the same time. You can't catch sight of a robin at close quarters in a park or on a woodland walk and not smile. That's why robins are good for you. The joy of robins, I call it.

Mind you, don't go getting the wrong impression. Just because this book is entitled 'The Magnificent British Garden Robin in HIS own words' it doesn't mean to say it's all about male robins exclusively. It certainly is not. Only *someone* from the robin community has to write a book like this – it's sorely needed – and it just so happens that I am a male of the species – and a rather handsome one too, as you can see from the many excellent illustrations a chap did for me the other day (I can't remember his name. It's probably on the back cover).

Anyway, for all these reasons and many more, I reckon this is just the sort of book you've been looking for. Give yourself a treat and come with me as I take you through a typical year in the life of robins. I'll tell you all about how we live; about how we build our nests and how we raise our young. I'll tell you about how we fight and defend our territory, and how we survive outdoors in all weathers. It really is a fascinating story – not only full of romance and song but also an astonishing amount of hardships and dangers.

Yes, *dangers*. It really is that scary. And I don't even know if I'll be able to get through to the end of writing all this before something terrible happens. We might well have been voted Britain's Favourite Bird just a few years ago and have millions of admirers all over the world, but that doesn't mean to say that life in the garden is exactly a bed of roses for robins. For a start, almost everything out here wants to eat us. Hawks, cats, foxes – the list of predators is endless. It's a precarious existence. And during a harsh winter we can get very hungry ourselves.

Not only that, but there's also a lot of misunderstanding concerning robins and our needs. It can be frustrating. For instance, when you lay down vast areas of paving or decking in your gardens instead of proper lawns with lots of juicy worms in them for us to eat, or when you put up the wrong types of nesting boxes and then expect us to use them when they're the wrong shape and they just don't suit our requirements at all.

Enough is enough, I say! Education is what's needed. In other words, if you're fond of robins, you have to read this book. If you *love* robins, you simply cannot do without it. It's chock–full of lots of practical ideas and useful information on what birds like us really want. So keep it handy for reference.

Right. That's the introduction done with. Now onto the chapters: one for each season. There're only four of those, the last time I counted – and because I have to type this very slowly, one letter at a time with my tiny beak, it's not going to be a long book.

We begin with winter.

Robin in Winter

WINTER

I must say there's a lot of peculiar ideas around at this time of the year concerning robins. As if winter just wouldn't be winter at all without a cute little red-breasted bird hopping up and down outside in the cold. People notice us more now I suppose because we do have those splendid orange-red feathers on our chests, and we do tend to be conspicuous in a dull garden setting. Yes, very nice I'm sure. All animated, cute and fluffy. But we don't go on like that for your benefit, y'know!

I shall explain why it is we have our magnificent red plumage later on. And there are lots of interesting stories attached to it. But for now, be assured winter is not exactly a walk in the park for birds like us, and we have to take our situation very seriously. Apart from rumours of one or two exceptionally fortunate robins who find themselves in demand posing as artists' models on Christmas cards, most of us out here in the real world have a pretty hard time of it, especially now during the grim and hungry months of winter. You see, even though we might be reluctant to admit it we really are quite vulnerable little creatures. Just take a look at these vital statistics, and you'll understand what I mean.

ROBIN'S VITAL STATISTICS

Old English colloquial name: The Redbreast

Latin name: Erithacus Rubecula

Colouring: olive brown with red breast & white belly

Typical Size: around 5 inches long (12.5 -14.0 cm)

Wingspan: between 8 and 9 inches (20 -22 cm)

Weight: around three quarters of an ounce (19.5 g)

The vital statistics of a typical adult robin

Appearances can be deceptive

What I'm trying to say is that although I might look all rotund and bonny when I fluff up my feathers it's easy to be deceived by appearances. Underneath all that covering, a robin is quite a tiny bird. We don't weigh much either, and so it really is a constant struggle for us to keep body and soul together.

Robins have a wide distribution here in the UK, and you can find us living just about everywhere – in woodland, on farms, in parks and gardens. Our habitat even extends to built-up areas and busy cities. Our European cousins, meanwhile, can be found as far north as the Arctic Circle and as far eastwards as Poland and Russia.

Our average life-span is less than two years. Yes, that is short, isn't it! This is because we are at our most vulnerable as youngsters during the first few months of life. Many robins perish at this early stage due to predation – that is, from other birds and creatures that want to eat us. But once that dangerous early period has been traversed, a robin can live a good few years. We can easily survive for anything up to eight years, and there is even an instance in Ireland of one reaching eleven!

Well, that's all very reassuring, I must say, but for me it still doesn't detract from the perils of the present, because this is winter, and one of the biggest causes of robin mortality is the cold.

Dealing with the cold

Yes, it really can be bitter cold at this time of the year in the UK, especially at nights – and certainly if you have to sleep outdoors, as all robins do of course. And the farther north in the UK a robin lives the greater the challenge becomes. There can be snow and blizzards – and freezing spells of weather that last not just for days but *weeks* – so that you might well wonder how small birds like us can survive at all. And if that wasn't enough, those dark, cold nights really do seem interminable – lasting for what could be anything up to 16 hours during December until the sun comes up each morning and we finally have an opportunity to look for something to eat.

A very cold night like that can result in a significant drain on our energy and fat reserves, during which we can easily lose up to 10% of our body weight just to keep ourselves going. How's that for an effective diet regime? Though I wouldn't recommend it out of choice. All too often the elderly robins among us fail to make it through a very cold night. They just go to sleep and don't wake up – and all that remains of them in the morning is a few scattered feathers after the fox has had his breakfast.

Oh, it might all look very nice on those cards and wrapping paper at Christmas – a pretty little red-breasted robin perched on a snow-covered branch with bells and tinsel in the background. But you try doing it – sitting up outside all night in the snow with a blustery wind whistling up the south-west approaches. The good news is that the younger and healthier a robin is the greater their tolerance of such conditions, and the typical hardships of winter that most of you reading this would baulk at and find unacceptable are usually no problem for a strong robin like me. So let me tell you how I do it.

Like most birds, robins have a surprisingly high body temperature – something that comes in handy later on in the year for encouraging the incubation of our eggs. We also have a pretty fast metabolism compared to many creatures, and our little hearts can beat much faster than yours – up to 1000 times per minute.

That certainly explains why humans seem to us robins

to be such remarkably slow, lumbering beasts – while from your point of view we always seem to be rushing around so quickly, always on the go, pecking away at things and eating. And it's true, we do eat a lot, especially when you consider our size. We have to keep those inner fires burning, you see. And in this respect, our internal workings really are remarkably versatile, so that when conditions become really severe we can slow things right down when we sleep. The blood flow to our extremities for example will become restricted at such times, which prevents vital body heat being wasted.

Legs and Feet

But what about those spindly little legs, I hear you ask? Yes, robins' legs are thin, aren't they! Though what you think are our legs are in fact really our feet, because robins have lovely long feet (not at all like people with your short little ones) and because of this our ankles are right up under our tummies.

Anyway, legs or feet, whatever you want to call them, they aren't exactly meaty, I'll give you that, and I can understand why you would assume they must get cold very easily. But if you look closely you'll notice that they are actually covered in numerous tiny scales that mitigate the loss of heat. We also have a particularly intricate network of blood vessels in our extremities – tiny interlaced arteries and veins all very close to one another, so as the warm blood flows down through our arteries it warms up the cool blood returning to our hearts via our veins. See how clever robins are?

We also shiver just like you do to help keep warm. And when we 'go to roost' and sleep, which we do standing up and normally perched on a branch or deep within a bush or thicket of some kind, we might even raise one leg for a while and tuck it up into our feathers. Then we'll put the leg down again on the branch and lift up the other one and do the same, so each one gets a turn in the warmth close to our bodies. That's clever too, isn't it!

By the way, don't go worrying about us falling off. The tendons of our feet tighten to a vice-like grip on our perches when we sleep, so we stay put even in a strong wind. I suppose it might be a bit different in a hurricane. That would be a rather extreme circumstance. A robin might well come to grief then and blow away. But I bet his legs and feet stay behind.

So you see, creatures like us out here in the wild will accept all the hardships that nature throws at us with a certain stoicism, even indifference, knowing we are built to withstand the majority of them. And though we will be glad when the bad weather ends, we don't have any fear of the cold or the wet, especially if our feathers are in tip-top condition, as any self-respecting robin will always make sure of. Which brings me to a very important topic indeed.

Fabulous Feathers

Marvellous things, feathers. Beautiful too. Robins are immensely proud of them. They don't only look good but they also come to the rescue in respect of the cold and in keeping our bodies dry. We have hundreds of them, and among these several different varieties, from the multitude of fine feathers on our faces and bodies, to the magnificent long flight feathers of our wings – which are, in fact, extensions of our arms and hands. We keep those folded at our sides when not flying, and they insulate our bodies perfectly – along with all the more soft, downy feathers found on our chest and flanks. This is the area that features our splendid red breasts, of course, and a pleasantly contrasting white area extending downwards to the underside. Unmistakable.

I'll have more to say about feathers a little later (see the section on moulting in Chapter 4). But for now, be assured, they really are amazing structures, each one composed of a multitude of the finest fibres all perfectly aligned and hooked together to form the typical elongated shapes most of you are familiar with.

That's why when the weather is chilly you'll see us robins fluffing up our feathers. The air caught between them insulates us brilliantly – rather like when you plump up one of those old-fashioned feather-down quilts you have on your beds. It can make us look funny, like a little round ball of fluff with a beak sticking out, but it does the job – it traps the warm air close to our skin and keeps us snug.

Not only that, but we make sure our faces and beaks can tuck in too when we sleep, all nuzzled up into the feathers on our shoulders. That way the air we breathe is warm too.

Typical wing feather

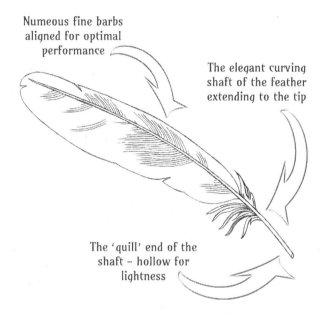

Numeous fine barbs
aligned for optimal
performance

The elegant curving
shaft of the feather
extending to the tip

The 'quill' end of the
shaft – hollow for
lightness

A flight feather from the wing

Our feathers also have a natural coating of oil, by the way, which we obtain from a special gland called the uropygial gland, situated on our backs at the base of our tails. This secretes an oily or waxy substance that not only provides additional insulation against the cold but also acts as the perfect water-proof coating for our plumage. It stays in place and holds good even in the driving rain, and therefore helps keep our skin underneath perfectly dry.

Design classic

Yes, we're designed well, us robins. We're just like a great piece of classic engineering – due to millions of years of natural selection, they reckon. And all these advantages combined mean that we can comfortably sleep outdoors, perfectly safe and warm in almost any weather. In fact, as you have probably gathered by now, robins could well be described as little bundles of heat on legs: like tiny furnaces out there in the night.

How does that poem go? *'Tyger, Tyger burning bright. In the forests of the night'*. I reckon it ought to be 'Robyn, Robyn, burning bright', don't you?

Robin roosting with holly and icicles

Anyway, now that you have discovered how brilliantly I regulate my temperature and keep warm even under the harshest conditions, what about when a hungry robin like me wakes up and gets cracking in the mornings? What do I feed on? And at this wretched time of the year how on earth do I even find anything to eat anyway when the ground is often frozen and hard and I might be up to my shoulders in snow?

Here, then, is what we look for by way of breakfast, and how we locate it. In other words, it's time to go a-hunting.

Food: a scarce resource in winter

Robins consume a wide variety of foods: caterpillars, centipedes, worms, invertebrates of all kinds: insects; aphids, flies and their larvae; small beetles and even ants. In short, if it's alive and wriggly robins will usually have an appetite for it, and the more lively it is the better. Whenever I see a nice wriggly worm, for instance, I become almost mesmerised with pleasure for a moment before I gobble it up.

Spiders, too, are usually most agreeable and tasty – only not too large, thank you. Consider for a moment how big one of those great spiders in your bathtub looks when you discover it. How do you think something like that appears to a tiny robin when it marches round the corner? *Enormous.* They definitely don't come quietly if you try to pick up one of those in your beak. Some of them can give you a nasty nip in return.

The vegetarian option

Unfortunately, during the worst days of winter, the stark reality is that many of these foods are simply not available – becoming more and more scarce as the season proceeds. The shortage becomes especially challenging if there's a hard frost or if the ground is covered in snow. A large proportion of worms tend to disappear then, deep into the soil. There are definitely no caterpillars to be found (they come along much later), and those spiders I told you about are also not so easy to locate right now – unless I happen to spot one hiding up under the eaves of a building or shed. But even that's a pretty rare occurrence in the depths of winter.

This is when the 'vegetarian' or fruity option becomes an attractive proposition, what with all those small seeds, berries and currants hanging around in the gardens and hedgerows. Although some can be a bit tough and indigestible, most of them are surprisingly tasty and they really can be a life saver. We always enjoy them in the autumn anyway when they first appear on the bushes and trees. They provide lots of sweetness, which becomes converted into fat reserves and consequently lots of energy – along with valuable vitamins and minerals to keep us well.

Problem is, just about every other creature out here is partial to them as well. Even worse, when we have seasonal migrants passing through. We had a flock of peculiar, starling-sized birds the other day (I think you call them waxwings) – dozens of them flying in from the north on route to the continent. They might well have already flown non-stop for miles and they're ravenous when they get here. It's terrifying to watch them because they can strip an entire bush bare within minutes.

'Show us the berries!' they say. And you can't reason with them. Then off they go again on their travels, bellies full. Never see them again.

So, what with one thing or another, by the time the worst of the winter months have rolled around, most of those succulent fruits that we were so looking forward to will already have vanished into the tummies of other hungry birds – while the chances of finding a nice branch of holly with all those bright red berries at Christmas is pretty remote too, if not impossible with folks taking them indoors for their festive decorations.

Just put yourself in my shoes for a moment. You've been eyeing up all those lovely tasty berries for weeks on end, waiting for them to ripen. 'Oh, they're coming along nicely,' you say to yourself. Then suddenly one morning someone comes by with a pair of secateurs, and they're gone. It's terribly disappointing. *Leave some for us, please!*

Yes, our culinary choices really do narrow dramatically as the season deepens and runs into the new year. Times are hard. And to put this into a human context, take a look at the following menu, indicating just what's available (and equally as important what's *not* available) for robins during a typical winter season:

The Hungry Robin
MENU

WINTER SEASONAL FARE

Earthworms (subject to availability)
Spiders (limited selection)
~~Caterpillars~~
~~Centipedes/millipedes~~
~~Maggots & grubs~~

VEGETARIAN

Berries (wild)
Plant and weed seeds (various)
~~Hedgerow Fruit~~

DESSERT

Secialities fresh from the bird table

Bread and biscuit crumbs
Mealworms
Bespoke Suet Creations (fatballs)
Finely chopped and moistened Sultanas

Opening times: sunrise to sunset daily.
Garden Lane, Wrigglesbury, Hunts, AR0 8IN

Winter season's menu at The Hungry Robin

Feeding off scraps – yes please!

Yes, hard times for birds, these winter months – unless, that is, a nice friendly person like you intervenes on our behalf. As you can see from the dessert section of our menu, readers of this book will make great friends with their local robins if they choose to leave out some scraps for us during the winter period.

In this context, bread is OK, and in extreme circumstances can mean the difference between life and death. But what we *really* want from you are treats like mealworms, which you can buy from most pet shops, garden centres or online. Usually these come in dried form (not at all wriggly, alas) – but you can make them more appetising by soaking them in water first. Almost as desirable as mealworms (in fact I personally prefer them) are dried fruits like raisins or sultanas – though again I always appreciate it if you can moisten them a little first, otherwise they can be a bit tough and hard to swallow. The occasional pinch of finely chopped cheese is often very welcome too.

And don't you go worrying about us putting on too much weight (chance would be a fine thing). It's not a matter of 'survival of the fittest' out here at this time of the year - it's *survival of the fattest* - that's what counts.

(See chapter three for lots more information on feeding robins.)

My song – loud and clear even in winter

So, after breakfast a robin will start to turn his attention to other equally important occupations, like singing. Yes, *singing* – it really is an essential aspect of a robin's life, a behaviour for which we are justly famed and celebrated. Whereas most other birds only put in the effort for a few months around the mating season, we can break into song just about any time. Rarely in Britain during the depths of winter will you hear too much birdsong, apart from ours: the tuneful and merry notes of robins.

I know, it might all seem a bit frivolous – singing at a difficult time like this, and a terrible waste of energy amid such austerity, but we love it. Even in the depths of a soggy winter, even when the ground is covered in snow and the icicles hang from every branch, still we will sing – and it really would have to be pretty awful out here, weather wise, to make us ever think of stopping. That's because as early as mid-winter we have already started demarcating our territory, a home patch where we will soon be pairing up with a robin of the opposite sex in readiness for the breeding season in spring. And singing is an essential part of attracting attention.

It's like a kind of advertisement and calling card combined, and a means of sounding a warning note too if necessary, signalling our willingness to defend our patch from other greedy robins who might be after any of that extra food we will soon be requiring for our growing family.

Mating – a partnership in prospect

Yes, mating. You can't get on with that sort of thing too soon, in my opinion. And that's why once the days begin to lengthen after Christmas we start getting all excited and looking forward to it. Yes, I know the weather can still be grim at this stage and there might well be plenty of cold days and nights ahead, but robins are optimistic, forward-looking creatures. And though we would much prefer just to concentrate on foraging and keeping ourselves alive under these conditions, unless we start to select a territory now and make it clear we are prepared to defend it, someone else will do it for us, and all the best plots will be gone. Not to mention all the best mates!

I should just add that we don't do anything physical yet by way of mating (and neither would you, I bet, outside in these sorts of temperatures) but we do succumb to a certain attraction and decide on who we are likely to join with, and then we'll begin to share our territory together in preparation for a little more intimacy later on. In other words, providing we have enough food to keep us going we can be happy with our lot, so that by January you might well find me already partnered up on a kind of provisional basis with a lady robin – all with an eye to raising a family later in the year. I'll be singing louder than ever then, you can rely on that – and even chasing away other male robins from our neck of the woods.

Setting our boundaries – and keeping them

Although winter undoubtedly has its hardships to contend with, it also has its opportunities, and its own special beauty – the noble gloom in the gardens, the silence of falling snow or the fantastic tangle of bare-branched trees – it all goes to remind us of our internal clock and calendar, of who we are and where we are going. We can get a good idea now of just how those trees and bushes are formed, and can imagine just how they will grow in time and how the leaves will cover them and give us shade and seclusion and – most importantly – how they can support nesting later on in the year and help us define the boundaries of our individual robin territories.

Maybe just now and then we might look back with a little nostalgia to times when the sun was warm and much higher in the sky – instead of a dim little disc (if you can see it at all!) But then only winter can give you those really fiery sunsets that break through late in the day, all crimson and frosty, lighting the bark of trees. It might make your eyes go all funny if you stare at it for too long, but a robin will observe that special kind of radiance with admiration because we like nothing so much in nature as bright colours – and red in particular gets us excited and just a little bit frisky and combative too – speaking of which, this is where things start to get really interesting.

Fighting – serious, but jolly good fun

Our personal territory can be anything up to an acre or two in size. That's large, isn't it – though never too large that we can't catch the singing of other birds in the distance and speculate on what they might be up to. To be honest, robins aren't all that bothered by the presence of other species of birds, but we are very particular about sharing our patch with other robins. We regard them as trespassers. That's why any resident robin worth his salt will know all about every other robin in his or her vicinity, even if we haven't made their acquaintance personally. And we achieve this understanding through song.

Trouble is, there really is an awful lot of misunderstanding concerning this kind of musicality - and of birdsong generally. It might all sound very pleasant and melodious to you, but to other robins, singing can be a herald to combat or at the very least an indication of our readiness to defend a territory with determination, all of which can be quite intimidating if you are another robin on the receiving end. And, just for the record, I should also add that the female robins can be every bit as formidable. They too sing in winter, and fight – *and how!* – as many a cocky male robin has discovered to his cost if he ever believed he could strut around inside a strong lady-robin's territory without invitation.

As for me? Well, normally, just a few robust melodies of an appropriately martial nature are sufficient to impress any would-be interlopers and make them think twice about encroaching on my home turf. But there are certain levels of persuasion in this respect. The process advances in various stages of escalating ferocity, and sometimes I have to go further than just singing.

Warning signals and display

Right – so this section is all about fighting, and that sounds thrilling, but what has to be taken into account is that there's a whole lot of tweeting and singing and ruffling of feathers that comes first and serves as a prelude to anything remotely like physical combat between rival robins. Fighting is a last resort.

To begin with, if I detect the song of a would-be intruder I'll sing back, and he (or she) will invariably answer too. It's all very civil, and it's good to know the other robin has its boundaries, just as I have mine. It's a kind of mutual respect. And I'm glad to tell you that in most instances disputes over territory are resolved amicably in this way. But if he gets a bit cheeky, the other chap, and comes too near to my part of the world, I'll then need to adopt extra measures.

This is when I'll fly up much closer to the boundary itself, so he can see for himself as well as hear just who's in charge in these parts and exactly what a magnificent specimen he's up against. Then I'll pipe up again, and even more vigorously than before, and he'll holler back in the same vein. The stand-off can go on for a good while, a sort of vocal *toing and froing*, and we can indeed come pretty close to exchanging blows at this stage. More often than not though the other robin will relent and return to his own patch without any fighting or bloodshed and all is well. But if not, then a proud robin like me has to consider the next step.

This is when things start to get really close and personal. I might well land right next to the other chap this time, perhaps even on the same branch or piece of ground, and then you'll see me really showing off. I'll start swaying from side to side – displaying my girth. It's a warning, clear and simple, demonstrating just how well built and strong I am. And if that doesn't impress him then I'll lift my head and thrust out my chest so as to display all those magnificent scarlet feathers of mine. I might even fly up in the air, almost vertical take off – then down again right in front of the other chap.

Well ... that really is pretty impressive, I'm sure you will agree. And normally, with a handsome fellow like me, this really is the end of the matter and sufficient to persuade the intruder to buzz off for good. But if after all this palaver the other chap still doesn't take the hint, *even now* ... well, there's only one alternative.

I'll attack.

The red mist

As you know, robins are notoriously bold and courageous. We don't have all those red feathers for nothing, y'know! Red – it's the colour of Mars, the god of war? Well, that suits us just fine actually because we don't take any prisoners when it comes to fighting. A flying thrust with those sharp-pointed talons at speed or even a peck or two to the head from the rapier beak of an angry robin can be lethal (well ... for another robin, that is). And when we get riled up and the red mist descends, as they say, there's just no stopping us.

I've heard it said that one or two really vicious robins will even peck away at a dead robin until there's not much left of his opponent at all. That'll teach him!

Of course, personally I wouldn't ever do anything really vile like that. I am quite a cultured and civilised sort of robin. But I must say it is tempting sometimes when other birds wind me up. It's that other scarlet breast that does it: the brazen statement of rivalry. It just gets me going somehow. Even if I see a red ball in the garden or someone walking by in a red jumper I can get all irritable and restless.

I even came over all aggressive the other day seeing my own reflection in the wing mirror of a car. I thought it was another robin and it took me ages before I realised my mistake. You feel so silly when that sort of thing happens, don't you? And it didn't half hurt my beak.

Combative robin with snowdrops

But don't robins sing because they're happy?

This is a frequently asked question. And I must say I do become perplexed at the kinds of answers some people come up with. The trouble is, in the olden days people used to be quite sentimental about birds. Some still are. And because it cheered them up when they heard birds singing, especially at the end of a miserable winter, they got it into their heads that the birds were the same – that all that singing was about being happy too in a daft, sentimental kind of way – until eventually serious people with education (who weren't daft or sentimental at all) began to get very upset and cross about it.

That's why nowadays experts who study birds insist that we only sing out of aggression, that it's all just about standing our ground against rival robins and fighting. Correct. What I can't understand though is why they think a robin can't be happy when it's standing its ground and fighting? Because we are! You see, robins are really just like the warriors and jousters of olden times, the martial arts enthusiasts of the bird world. And me – I love making a song and dance and puffing out my red chest and jumping up and down and defending my patch. I love competing. And I love winning too. Never happier.

So, there you have it. You heard it here first. Don't let anyone try to convince you that we robins don't sing because we're happy. Of course we're happy! It's just like you always thought it was before clever people started to interfere.

Anyway, enough of all this violence. It's probably time for a drink. Water, naturally.

Water and the humble birdbath

Robins, like most other creatures, need to keep themselves properly hydrated: it's an all-year-round necessity. The problem is that fresh water can be one of the things we miss out on during icy conditions every bit as much as in the hot weather. And when the ponds and streams are frozen over and there are icicles hanging from every branch, water of any decent quality is not easy to find. That's where you, the owners of gardens have such an important role to play. Here are some tips on what you can do – beginning with what is surely one of the greatest inventions of humankind, and certainly one of my favourite pieces of garden architecture: the humble birdbath.

Birdbaths come in all shapes and sizes, from an upturned dustbin lid on the ground filled with fresh water right up to those ornate, elaborately crafted ones on plinths that you can shop for in garden centres. Strange as it might seem, the former is equally as good as the latter from the perspective of a thirsty robin. As long as it contains clean water and is perhaps raised a little above the ground to give us more protection when we visit, we aren't too fussed over what it looks like.

I'll tell you about how to maintain a suitable birdbath in a moment, but first let me explain in a little more detail just why a fresh supply of water is so important for us robins: because it's not just about drinking. A good birdbath properly maintained can also be a place that provides us with somewhere safe to take a dip and to get our feathers wet. This is important because bathing aids us in the essential business of preening, which in turn ensures we keep our plumage and flight feathers in tip-top condition. So, due to this unusual combination of needs, drinking and bathing, it goes without saying that having the water replenished regularly is paramount to the welfare of the birds who use it. Nothing to do with vanity, I'll have you know (as if a robin could ever be accused of such a thing) but rather as an essential aid in the daily business of survival. Let's look at this in more detail.

Preening those magnificent feathers

So what exactly is preening? Well, you will appreciate by this stage how important feathers are for a proud robin like me. Not only does my plumage make for the resplendent specimen of *robinhood* you would expect to see in any proper British garden, with a red breast and a fine little fluffy white tummy, but it's also the means by which I keep dry, keep warm and take to the air and fly. And following a visit to the that well-maintained birdbath of yours, and with my feathers suitably moistened, I can then flutter off to an adjacent perch and get to work on caring for them straight away. That's when you will see me progressing through all kinds of amazing contortions and stretches as I probe and run my beak through all my major feathers, especially the flight feathers on my wings, each of which I attend to individually and with great care.

In particular, you'll observe me reach around with my beak to a place on the lower back just at the base of my tail because it's here, you might recall, that the uropygial gland is situated. I can avail myself of some of that special oil here that is so essential for the vital process of robin grooming and for advanced feather care. This, I will then trail through my feathers, nibbling and stroking along the way, a process which not only removes lots of unpleasant dust and dirt but also encourages the fine interlacing structure of each feather to align itself correctly.

If you care to pick up a stray feather from the ground and examine it you will discover how it's made up of a substantial network of individual fibres running in parallel to one another. See the illustration on page 14. These are called barbs and collectively they form a smooth, aerodynamic surface by hooking onto one another. When I preen, I encourage all these tiny 'hooks' to engage correctly and thus ensure a good shape and texture to my wings. Yes, it might all sound a bit self-indulgent, I know, but work of this kind really is crucial for keeping our outer layers water-tight and for ensuring optimal flight performance, which in an emergency, say when a nasty predator might be about to pounce, might well prove the difference between escaping or getting caught. Preening has to be a daily routine, as well – in fact even more frequently by choice for a healthy bird.

So now you know just how important bathing is, here are some pointers to the essential make-up and qualities of a good birdbath – at least from a robin's perspective.

As you can see from the following illustration, the main requirement is that it be bowl-like and shallow, with gently sloping sides. A diameter of around 15 inches is ideal for most small birds, and with a generous edge to it, useful for perching on so we can take a good look around before we take the plunge.

The surface inside should not be too smooth, however, because that might cause us to slip and hurt ourselves. Meanwhile, the plinth or column beneath should be sturdy and serve the purpose of raising the bowl itself safely away from the ground. All this provides a most agreeable sense of security.

Whatever container or receptacle you use to fashion a birdbath, do please make sure that the water itself is not too deep. Remember, a robin is not a particularly large bird and none of us can swim. That's why we have to avoid places with steep sides. Lots of small birds drown in ponds each year when they paddle into water and get out of their depth. So if you want to see me or other birds in your garden on a regular basis making a splash, make sure the water is no deeper than a couple of inches please. That'll do nicely.

The Anatomy of a Birdbath

A broad basin with sloping sides sufficiently wide for splashing about in while being also easily lifted off for cleaning.

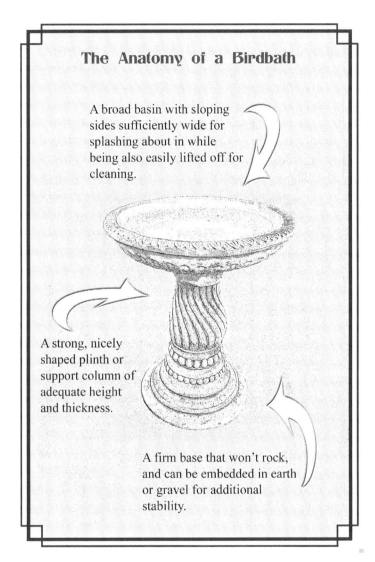

A strong, nicely shaped plinth or support column of adequate height and thickness.

A firm base that won't rock, and can be embedded in earth or gravel for additional stability.

The ideal birdbath from a robin's point of view

Birdbath Location

It's best to situate the birdbath in a fairly open aspect, away from any bushes where predators such as cats might be lurking. It's also helpful if you can place it in a sunny spot, as the sunlight helps reduce the spread of algae and bacteria in the water, while in winter it might also reduce the likelihood of the water freezing over during the day.

Whatever facility you arrange for us, it goes without saying that it should be inspected regularly. If necessary, remove any icy crust by breaking the surface in the mornings or, if the water is frozen solid, try pouring a little warm water on top to thaw it. Only do make sure the water isn't too hot please. The sudden change might well crack your birdbath if it's too hot, and it could hurt us anyway if we suddenly jump in.

Best of all is to change the water regularly, so it is always fresh and that it is therefore also disease free. Dirty water can be very dangerous to birds – there being certain bacteria or viruses lurking in foul or stagnant water that can make us sick, and an unhealthy bird can also pass on its diseases to other birds who drink after.

This, I should add, is not just a matter of welfare: it's aesthetics. Imagine if you had to drink water in which most of your neighbourhood had already been wallowing in? You wouldn't fancy that, would you? Well, robins face a similar predicament. Me, I am actually quite a fastidious bird, and I'm not at all keen on drinking water after all those dirty crows or pigeons have been paddling about and clearing their throats in it for days. Worse, some of those birds are very careless and might even do a *whoopsie* in the water before they fly off. That's just disgusting in my opinion. You'd have to be pretty desperate, I can tell you, to drink from a birdbath in that state. But sometimes there's no other choice. *Yuk!*

So yes, I suppose I really ought to 'come clean' here and admit to a certain degree of vanity after all because if I am well groomed and looking my best it does impress other robins. Especially useful for attracting a mate or for those vital territorial displays. Getting rid of the daily detritus in this way is also a most agreeable sensation – a great pleasure in fact. In other words, robins need you! We need you to take charge of the birdbath and its maintenance. Are you ready to become a Knight of the order of the Birdbath and go into battle against all those horrid microbes and germs? Good. Here is a handy guide on how to set about it.

Birdbath hygiene – modus operandi

The first step to cleaning the bath is to get rid of all the old water – making sure you do so in a place where it will soak away immediately and where birds won't simply come along and try to bathe in it some more! Being most likely quite mucky, this can actually be beneficial to garden plants (a bit like liquid manure).

BIRDBATH WARRIORS
THE ESSENTIAL KIT

You will need ...

A little drop of household bleach containing chlorine.

Rubber gloves and protective goggles for your safety.

A small bucket or bowl to mix up bleach: 1 part to 10 parts hot water.

Some wire-wool for stubborn grime, or a sturdy old washing-up brush (not one currently in use).

Plenty of fresh water for rinsing afterwards. Rinse, rinse and rinse again.

The birdbath-warrior's cleaning kit

Commence cleaning of the birdbath using a mild solution of a little household bleach mixed to about ten parts warm water. Gloves and goggles are recommended for this, because you don't want to be getting any of that yucky stuff in your eyes. Don't incorporate any other chemicals.

Use an old washing up brush or suchlike to clean away any debris or mess from the bottom and around the edges too, bearing in mind that here is where birds will land and perch initially and probably stand on too for a moment after bathing before taking off again. Have some wire wool handy, or a wire brush for removing any hard or stubborn lumps or encrustations.

Splendid! At the end of the exercise, rinse thoroughly to make sure there are no residues of diluted bleach remaining. This is very important because bleach is not good for the little tummies of birds like me. Also, remember that delicate waxy coating we have on our feathers? The last thing that needs is traces of bleach in our bathing water. So please remember to rinse, rinse and rinse again, disposing of the liquid safely, before finally filling up the birdbath with fresh water from a hose or watering can, which should obviously also be squeaky clean and not have been used for any hazardous garden chemicals.

You don't need to undertake a major cleanse of the birdbath like this every day, of course, or even every week, but do make the effort occasionally. And then your robins will reward you by staying healthy and beautiful all year round. A real feather in your cap, I'd say.

Reliability

Finally, I would not be a responsible robin if I did not take this opportunity to remind you about the issue of reliability. Birds will come to depend on your splendid birdbath, but this can sometimes do more harm than good if it's not replenished regularly or if it suddenly fails to provide any water at all. Birds are creatures of habit, and we can waste a lot of vital energy searching out alternatives if our regular source of water has suddenly dried up when you go away on holiday for several weeks. Ask a neighbour to take responsibility if you cannot tend to the birdbath yourself for any length of time.

So, in conclusion, the birdbath is great – but only *truly great* if you maintain it and keep it topped up and clean for us. If you miss out, even if just for a day or two, especially in extreme conditions, it can be very distressing. Don't let us down!

Naming of the Robin – a rich history

Here in the UK there has always been a long and rich history of association between robins and people. Over the centuries, we have entered the thoughts and emotions of humans in a way no other bird has quite been able to do, and a fascinating blend of folklore, legend and mythology has grown up around us. In particular, the various different names you have given to us have altered quite a bit, and this can reveal a lot about the evolution of ideas and attitudes concerning your favourite bird. Very early on, for example, in Anglo-Saxon Britain, we were given the name of ruddock. And it was only later in the Middle Ages when folks began to call us the redbreast. Both these names reflect the warm red or *ruddy* colour of our chest. Our most salient feature.

By Tudor times people were beginning to add pet names, diminutives of Christian names before the regular titles of birds, so 'Jenny' was placed before Wren, or 'Robin' before the Redbreast – so *Robin Redbreast* became our popular name, and that remained the case right up until the Victorian era here in Britain. 'Robin' is a diminutive deriving from the name *Robert,* which in itself means something like 'bright fame'. This, in turn, hails from continental Europe, brought over to Britain by the Normans in the far-away 11th century. But it wasn't applied to us birds until much later.

Incidentally, there was a brief spell during Elizabethan times when we were also called Robinets. But that dropped out of favour quickly.

So, back to our story: what happened to our name in Victorian times? Well, it's all to do with the postal service and with letters and parcels. When, in the 19th century, the Royal Mail introduced the Penny Post, it suddenly became far more convenient and affordable for folks to send greeting cards to one another, especially ahead of important occasions such as Christmas or Easter. The printing costs for cards were also coming down about this time too, so little tokens like these became a popular way of keeping in touch. In those days the postmen who delivered them wore bright red coats, and they soon became fondly nicknamed *redbreasts* or *robins*. Colourful images of robins both as bird and man also started to appear on cards at this time. And it was shortly after this when we stopped being called robin redbreasts, and instead became just 'robins'.

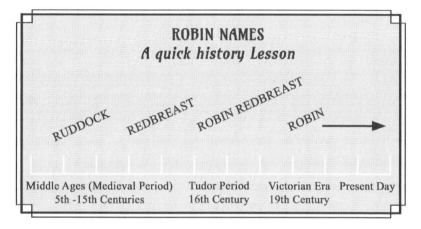

ROBIN NAMES
A quick history Lesson

RUDDOCK   REDBREAST   ROBIN REDBREAST   ROBIN

| Middle Ages (Medieval Period) 5th -15th Centuries | Tudor Period 16th Century | Victorian Era 19th Century | Present Day |

Robin names – an approximate timeline

Robin – the legend

But there's more to us than just a name, of course. There have been, and still are, lots of interesting tales and symbolic associations to consider. These have ancient origins and are really most fascinating if I say so myself. And naturally many of these revolve around legends concerning just how we got our magnificent and rightly celebrated scarlet plumage.

There is an Irish folk tale for instance, concerning a year in which there was a very harsh winter with thick snow on the ground and the birds were facing starvation. So they all got together and asked the robin, who was known to be the bravest of them all, to go to the farmer and ask if he could leave out some crumbs occasionally so the birds might have something to keep them going. The farmer agreed, and the birds survived. Well done robin! All the other birds were so pleased that in gratitude they knitted him a little red waistcoat. And that's how we became the fine red-breasted bird of today.

Redeeming Robins

There is also a fair bit of Christian symbolism associated with robins, and again with the focus very much on our red breasts. It's said that we used to be just a dull, brown sort of bird until the blood of Christ, pierced by his crown of thorns, fell onto us. The robin itself at the time was endeavouring to remove one of the horrid thorns with its beak: a noble and courageous gesture. So from that day forth robins came to be seen as heroic and merciful creatures, and we had our resplendent red-robin plumage covering our hearts to proclaim as much to the whole world.

Later on, the painters and artists of the Victorian era took special notice of us and would often place us in their paintings, precisely because of this redeeming feature, sometimes depicting wounded, captive or dead robins as a symbol of sacrifice or even of the Crucifixion itself.

That's a bit depressing, isn't it? *Victorians.*

One welcome outcome to emerge from this rich vein of symbolism, though, is because we have come to be renowned for so many noble qualities, for our courage and mercy, there are lots of instances in English folklore that warn against harming us robins – that it will surely curdle the milk or bring bad luck or even death to any person reckless enough to do so. That's a good idea in my view and I support it wholeheartedly.

Babes in the Wood

Our fine reputation has also been further enhanced by the legend that a robin, if it comes across the body of someone who has died, will cover their eyes with moss or leaves. Much of this stems from a popular 16th-century folk tale, 'The Babes in the Wood' – a story of two innocents who, at the behest of their wicked uncle, are abducted and abandoned in the forest where they die. So once again, robins appear as noble-spirited and compassionate birds.

> *No burial these prettye babes*
> *Of any man receives,*
> *Till Robin-redbreast painfully*
> *Did cover them with leaves.*

Not everyone believes that, but I can tell you this: some of us robins will cover our shiny eggs with moss or leaves to stop them being too conspicuous. And no doubt some would do the same for any creature they find exposed in such a pitiful state.

More recent pantomime adaptations of the tale at Christmas have happier endings, and on stage the babes are rescued by none other than Maid Marion and Robin Hood. Robins just cannot escape Christmas can they! (Nor would we ever wish to).

Anyway, the upshot of all this is that robins just wouldn't be called robins, if it wasn't for all these stories and associations merging and coming together, because of letters and legends and postmen and faith and Christmas. And although it's almost impossible to disentangle one from the other, it's people like you and your ideas that have made robins what we are today. Not only that, but in a funny sort of way its robins that have made you what you are too.

Cor! Makes you think, doesn't it!

On with the rest of the day

Anyway, what next? I've told you about what we eat and what we get up to at the start of each morning, but what about the remainder of the day? How do robins pass their time until the evening? Well, the simple answer is that we keep on eating, and lots of it if we can. That's because we need to ensure a healthy store of fat in preparation for that long, cold night ahead. Once we go to sleep we invariably stay put. There's no getting up for a nice little midnight snack for a robin (honestly, sometimes I could *murder* a worm). So during these limited daylight hours, we need to take on as much warming nourishment as we can, and to be perfectly honest that takes up pretty much all our attention.

There is one exception though, and one activity that occupies our time a little more now and becomes more and more appealing to a robin as the winter proceeds into the new year, and this is where it all starts to get even more exciting. What am I referring to? I'm talking about searching for love.

The late-winter romancing period

As I believe I mentioned earlier, by the time Christmas arrives we've already been singing vigorously for some time, but now with the lengthening days of the new year we find ourselves piping up louder and more melodiously than ever. This is because something really magical begins to take place once the shortest days and the longest nights have passed. Just look at the garden and you'll understand immediately – what with all those curly fronds of new bracken and the green of wild garlic plants that seem to spring up almost overnight. There's just so much energy about!

And suddenly you notice all those empty branches are covered now in tiny buds, all silky and oily and wanting to burst into leaf and blossom. And robins are the same. Instead of struggling to survive on meagre rations, there's a little more food about now and we also have lots of energy. It makes you feel you want to be done with winter – to get cracking and to just *do things*. We might not exactly know what it is we want to do at first, especially the younger and less experienced robins, but there's definitely a sense of promise in the air. This is in fact the approach of the nesting season, which although it can commence as early as February, will take place more typically in March or April. And the prospect of it makes a robin feel quite buoyant.

Funny, too, the alteration in the way we look at other robins at this time. Whereas during the start of winter we were at each other's throats most of the time, male and female alike, threatening and warning each other off our territories and singing and fighting, now suddenly one or two of those other robins start to look ... well, strangely beguiling.

Mrs Robin appears

It can happen quite swiftly and unexpectedly, and it's a bit of shock when it does. One robin in particular will start to look really attractive – in fact *beautiful*. That's the only way I can describe it. They do say beauty is in the eye of the beholder, don't they? And I'm sure that's true, because I find myself getting all amorous when I catch sight of my robin partner – the 'hen' as you might call her in academic circles but whom I shall refer to from here on in as Mrs Robin. That's far more respectful in my opinion for such a gorgeous bird. (*Hen?* Like something you'd find running around in a farmyard.)

Which brings me to a frequently asked question: is there an easy way to distinguish gender, the difference between male and female robins?

No, is the simple answer – unless you are another robin, that is – while experts on birds who observe us in the wild have concluded with great reluctance that there is just no way of doing so with any reliability. Both of us, male and female, have red breasts, and we are both about the same size. Sometimes, within a pair of robins, the female might be a tad larger. But, there again, also sometimes smaller. Occasionally, you'll hear people say that the male will have a little white bar stripe on the edge of his wing. But then, frustratingly, *sometimes not.*

But of course it really is easy in my opinion to tell the difference because lady robins are so much more lovely. And though I'll concede it's probably not at all scientific, that's how I tell the difference. Not only that, but I'm convinced my Mrs Robin is the most lovely of all – and (to tell you a secret) I can't really believe that anyone that lovely could ever fancy me at all. But there you are: that's romance for you. And I'm not complaining.

Fidelity? Well, not exactly

In some respects, robins are similar to people in their mating habits. Some pair up and stay together for ages, even for life, while others are inclined to – let me put this delicately – indulge in 'open relationships'. Female robins, moreover, are just as likely to stray from the straight and narrow as male ones, especially if a younger, more virile male comes onto the scene. It quite turns their heads.

Male robins, meanwhile, face a bit of a quandary at the end of the winter months because a whole new bunch of female robins who might have migrated overseas for the winter are suddenly back with us again. It's the female robins who are the more likely to migrate you see. And so it's a real joy for us when they return home (I'll tell you more about that later on in the chapter on autumn).

Naturally, all this can prove unsettling and confusing for some of the younger and more promiscuous male robins who at the best of times just don't know when to rein in their desires. The result is that they can finish up with two females on the go at once – bigamy, as the behaviour is correctly termed – and which can become a major inconvenience if the two females happen to nest at similar times. Oh dear! The reckless robin in question will then be compelled to rush about sustaining two families at once, with two separate batches of ravenous chicks growing up and wanting attention. Exhausting it is. (Not that I have any experience of that kind of predicament myself, you understand. *Ahem*).

So there you have it. The weather might be rotten, and it might have been freezing and raining every day and utterly miserable and dark, but by the time the winter comes to an end some robins have already been getting to work forming relationships that will last throughout the spring and well into summer, right through the nesting season and even beyond.

Winter – what winter? Little devils. I told you robins have a high body temperature didn't I? *Robins are hot* – and all that singing and fighting that we've been doing has not been in vain.

Spring really is on the way. And we are going to be so busy! You just wait and see.

Robin in Spring

SPRING

Spring: that magical season of lengthening days and joyful singing. It's just so exciting! Blustery winds and showers reaching into even the dustiest corners of the garden – it somehow spruces everything up, polishing the bark of the trees, and even the old holly and ivy leaves get a shine. There's white blossom breaking out everywhere – the blackthorn and hawthorn – and the fresh green of ash-tree leaves and the bronze of garden beech, and all those fluffy, nodding catkins on the willows too.

Um ... unfortunate name, that, by the way, don't you think? *Catkins.* I suppose it's because they are all soft and whiskery when you touch them, rather like the fur on a cat. Ugh! Makes the feathers on the back of your neck stand on end just thinking about it. Not that I'm going to dwell too much on unpleasant associations like that, because at this time of the year robins are full of good cheer and vigour. Nothing much can bother us because everything seems to feel good inside. It's like all your joints and feathers are in tip-top condition and even the older robins, like me, who've been knocking about for a year or two start to feel youthful and frisky once again. These are the days when you see me on the wing really showing off, executing the most spectacular acrobatics – flying this way and that, turning brilliantly in the air or else darting head-long into seemingly impenetrable bushes before jumping about like a jack-in-the-box on all the branches and trees. Typically, I like to survey things from a favourite perch or two high above ground – from which I will then swoop down onto anything that looks tasty and then, almost as if I'm on springs, darting quickly back up again in a flash.

Why, I can even hover in mid-air, stationary for a moment like one of those colourful exotic birds from far away places – what do you call them, *hummingbirds?* – and pick off things to eat from the most difficult places. My wings really are that strong.

But it's not just about being flash on the wing. It's also a time to strut about on the lawns. Now is when you'll see me flexing my tail, over and over again, stretching my neck high and dropping my wing feathers to look really tall. That, or else hopping or bobbing up and down on those strong ankles of mine – just to make sure, if anyone's looking (another robin especially) that they know exactly who's in charge around here.

A real swagger, that's me.

Fulfilling our relationship

Yes, it's a wonderful time of the year – not least because for so many creatures in the wild like us it's the season for finding a mate and raising a family. For birds this means building a nest, of course – or, to be more accurate in my case, watching Mrs Robin building one. Yes, it's always the female robin who builds the nest, who looks after it and sits on the eggs for days on end – thereby freeing off the male robin to spend more time on the important occupation of singing. I'll come to that entire process shortly and explain exactly how it works, the 'specialised division of labour between the sexes' as I like to call it (Mrs Robin doesn't call it that, by the way, but I'd rather not elaborate on that just at the moment).

Spring officially begins at the start of March by most folks reckoning – though robins are a bit different. As I stated towards the end of the last chapter, we tend to think of the romancing season (that is getting together and making baby robins) as coming a little earlier than that. Having by this time already partnered up we can be observed venturing upon the mating procedure and even nesting as early as February – especially if it feels like an early spring is imminent with ample food supplies for all those young robins that might be on the way. And although most nesting occurs more typically around April to June, even now, even when spring has hardly got its boots on, it's already time for fulfilling the promise of that early relationship.

A truce is called

Yes, it's romance. You just know it's right somehow. Take me and my Mrs Robin as an example. Having got over the shock of wanting to be friends instead of fighting each other as we were doing during the earliest days of winter, the two of us have already agreed to a kind of truce that will last for a good few months to come. Oddly, we don't feel aggressive to each other at all now and – even more oddly – we find ourselves spending lots of time together, following each other around the garden. We watch out for each other too if there's any danger about, and we even start to share morsels of food as tokens of friendship. This, by the way, is a very important courtship ritual, exchanging food. You'll notice it regularly among robins at this time of the year if you keep your eyes peeled, so I'd better describe the process in a little more detail and perhaps dispel a few misunderstandings.

Rituals of Courtship

People do often jump to the wrong conclusion when they spot a red-breasted robin feeding another at this time of the year. They assume it's a parent feeding its young. But that is not the case. It will be weeks yet before there are any baby robins hopping about in your gardens, and they don't have any red plumage anyway. Instead, what you see at this early stage of the season is one adult robin, invariably an amorous male like me, presenting items of food to an adult female. Yes, the male to the female. Never the other way around, which is rather a pity, but never mind. This is in fact a common pre-nuptial custom that will be repeated again and again over the days and weeks ahead, and both participants really enjoy it, especially when a male robin approaches his female with a nice wriggly worm or spider to pop into her beak. The female robin, though perfectly capable of feeding herself, finds this prospect incredibly amusing and she will flutter her wings and jump up and down with excitement, very similar to how young nestling robins behave when bidding for food. She will also often make the same sorts of baby-robin noises that they will make later on.

So, you see, ultimately it's eating that we relish the most in the courtship process. By contrast, copulation, the actual physical process of mating is rather a quick affair among robins. The male mounts the female robin and it's all over in a flash. But the feeding rituals associated with pairing up go on much longer and are repeated many times a day all through the spring and summer months. It's what really *flutters our feathers* so to speak and gets us in the mood.

In fact, a female robin might well accept as much as a third of all her food from her partner during this period. And even when they are not particularly hungry, our lady robins will still sidle up to us males and coax us into feeding them.

They love it. And we love it too!

Robin's courtship feeding

Nutritional demands for nesting

As a ritual, courtship feeding does make sense though when you come to think about it – what with all that extra energy and stamina needed for a female robin to build a nest and carry great heavy bunches of leaves and moss from place to place for the bedding – not to mention all those extra nutritional demands like additional calcium for the shells of the eggs. It stands to reason that she is going to require plenty of extra sustenance – after which, all being well, she will typically lay around four to six eggs in a period of a little under one week and which, taken altogether could weigh–in at around three quarters of her own body weight.

Yes, it is amazing, isn't it. She might well undertake this process two or three times during the nesting season. So the food I bring her at this time is a real turn on and that's why robins seem far more enamoured of it than the actual mating procedure itself – which, as I mentioned, is not only comparatively swift but also very different in a practical sense to humans and mammals. And if you can contain your excitement just a little longer, I'll tell you much more about that in a moment.

Meanwhile, there is just something else I have to be getting on with now that has to be repeated again and again throughout the course of the day, a very important occupation that we have touched upon already, of course, namely singing.

My song in spring

Yes, at this time of the year it is usually the male robins who take responsibility for most of the vocal parts. Some females continue to have a go at it, but they seem to lose their voices now and they haven't quite got the gusto and purpose that us males have. In fairness, they have other things to be doing with their energies. So we do understand.

The song itself, meanwhile, and though it continues to serve the purpose of establishing territorial boundaries as it did in winter, has an added urgency to it because I certainly don't want anyone else making eyes at my Mrs Robin, not at this delicate juncture. All those other robins singing from the trees yonder – they might be lonely bachelors for all I know. So I need to make sure they learn exactly who's the governor in this neck of the woods and who's finally got the girl. Mrs Robin, listening and looking out from her nest, finds all this very impressive by the way (at least I think she does). Robins are great romantics, y'know, and a male robin in full voice is a very attractive proposition to your average female robin.

But it's not all romance and extravagant gestures. I do a lot of practical things too at the moment – darting about from place to place for instance. It gives me a chance to explore all those amazing changes occurring in the garden. Look! You just can't count the number of tiny flowering plants that are bursting into bloom: the snowdrops, the daffodils and crocuses and all those little violets and yellow primrose things. There hardly seems enough space on the ground for them all sometimes. And there's cherry blossom, and the bluebell woods carpeted with great drifts of colour now where just a few weeks ago there was really nothing much to see at all.

There are new sounds also. The other birds like the thrushes and blackbirds are singing as loudly as I do. What a cacophony! Only just occasionally do you catch an off-note: the exceptionally *odd* call of the cuckoo. That's ominous. We have to be careful of those lazy birds because they are the ones who can lay their eggs in our nest and then fly off and expect us to do all the hard work feeding their young for them. What a cheek!

Anyway, back to the business in hand. I still have to keep an eye on Mrs Robin and make sure she continues to receive those little foody presents that I pick up for her. It's important that we two continue to bond like this you see, because one way or another there's quite a lot of work ahead. In fact, I would imagine if your average rookie robin knew just how much hard graft was in store at this time of the year, what with all the nesting and rearing the young, they might well have second thoughts about getting involved at all. But there you are. Love makes the world go round, they say. That's certainly true for robins, and once committed like this we tend to be loyal to each another throughout the season in order to get things done.

The nesting site is located

It's amazing really, this matting lark. It all happens naturally. And before you know it, one morning when I'm just about to pop a nice shiny beetle into Mrs Robin's beak she informs me that she's already located the perfect nesting site and wants to make babies!

Well, I don't mind the making-babies part of the arrangement. That suits my natural inclinations just perfectly as it happens. But as for building a complicated nest – all that straw and moss and so on – well, as I mentioned earlier I'm not cut out for that kind of work at all. In other words if you see an eager and sprightly robin gathering up leaves and moss in the garden and flying off with a beakful to some hidden location to make a nest, that'll be a Mrs Robin, never a Mr. The female can even become quite secretive about the process, moreover, and in my experience doesn't really like to be observed at all until it's all over and the nest is complete.

If you think about it, there are very good reasons for this. She doesn't want to draw attention to herself or the nesting site she has chosen in case any nearby predators might be observing her. That's understandable, I suppose – but she even gets stroppy sometimes if *I* come near. She tells me off!

Oh well ... I'm happy to let her get on with it. But even this does not mark the full extent of the male robin's detachment from the process of nesting, because by the same token it's also the female robin who will eventually sit on the eggs and incubate them. Never the male. I wish

I could give you a plausible explanation as to why this is the case by saying something like the underside of your typical male robin is just not designed for sitting on hard spherical objects. But that would be wrong of me, because male robins don't have anything like that underneath at all. No, *really*. Birds in general aren't built like mammals and we have an alternative arrangement for achieving reproduction.

Privy parts. An explanation of some delicacy

Birds do still have the same internal organs as you humans do. Females have ovaries and a uterus, and males have testes and seminal vesicles, but the difference with us is it's all on the inside and, notably in the case of us males, without any dangly bits. After all, it could prove rather impractical, don't you think – flying around through all those bushes with the 'undercarriage' down, so to speak. Instead, both male and female have what is called a 'cloaca' – an internal chamber with an opening on our bottoms to the outside. Both male and female cloacae are very similar, by the way.

So, if male robins don't have external genitalia, how, you may ask, do male and female actually mate? Well, it's all down to what is called the 'cloacal kiss'.

Sounds interesting? I'll explain.

Sex – yes, but probably not as you know it

When it comes to copulation the male perches on the back of the female briefly and she will move her tail feathers gently to one side allowing the male cloaca and female cloaca to come into contact. It is during this fleeting moment of intimacy, the cloacal kiss, that the male sperm is deposited, after which it journeys along the internal chamber of the female cloaca to fertilise an egg. This will eventually grow to form a soft shell, travelling in the other direction to be discharged through the orifice of her cloaca.

Voila! An egg is laid! It's all clever stuff. And not only that, but the same channel serves us in expelling urine and faecal matter as well. So yes, quite a versatile organ and all very different to the way you humans are put together. Personally, I think it's preferable and quite a handy arrangement, having everything in the same place like this. But you might disagree.

By the way, a robin's testes will increase in size dramatically, by a factor of hundreds at this time of the year, so you definitely sense something unusual is happening. Also, both male and female will have relatively large and distended cloacae, so the contact between them is not difficult – though like most things in life practice makes perfect. By this means, we endeavour to make an egg each day until Mrs Robin has laid a full complement in her nest. She will then begin to sit on them and the lengthy process of incubation can commence.

The Special Female Brood Patch

Most birds naturally lose their feathers at certain times – a process called moulting, and I shall tell you about that later in those chapters concerning summer and autumn. But for female robins at this time of the year, an early albeit modest loss of feathers occurs on the abdomen. The resulting bald patch during the mating and nest-building season is not easily visible under normal circumstances, but it does serve a very useful purpose when the female robin is sitting on her eggs and incubating them because it allows the warmth of her body to come in direct contact with the surface of the eggs.

Warmth is vital to the incubation process, encouraging the embryonic robins within the egg shells to grow into proper little birds-to-be who in a couple of weeks will eventually peck and break through the shells from inside. The brood patch helps things along splendidly in this respect. And the same principle continues to be applied to the hatchlings – the mother robin spreading her wings and keeping them warm in much the same way by sitting close to or on top of them – the process of brooding, as it is termed. By the way, don't worry, those abdominal feathers grow back to cover the bare patch later in the year – otherwise I suppose it would be rather chilly in the winter.

And so here at last, despite me assuring you earlier that it is almost impossible to determine the difference between the sexes, here is a pretty reliable way of distinguishing between male and female robins after all, at least for these few specific months of the year. Just check for the brood patch in spring.

Luckily, us male robins don't have to worry about that sort of thing – nor the indignity of having our tummies inspected by curious ornithologists. It is they who reveal the partly concealed patch by capturing a female robin, holding her gently upside down and blowing on her tummy. Well, that sounds a bit weird, if you ask me. But one or two robins I've spoken to say they actually quite enjoy it!

Moving on ...

Nesting – the where and the how of it

Robins, like most birds, are fussy about where they build their nests – these being wonderfully practical constructions, by the way, circular in form and open at the top like a bowl. The location for it has to be 'just right' – not too hot; not too cold; not too damp, and not too windy or prone to accidental movement that might expose it. Above all else it has to be *safe.*

This last stipulation is a major consideration, because there are all sorts of monsters out here who will eat robin eggs if they take a fancy to them. Squirrels, jays and magpies, badgers and foxes – I'll tell you all about these later on, don't worry. But they can prove a real headache for us so the nest that Mrs Robin builds has to be somewhere discreet and out of sight. That's why, in the wild, our females make their nests in bushes or thickets, and we don't mind if it's all a bit prickly either, like with hawthorn or holly, because that keeps many a nasty predator at bay.

I should just add here that small birds like us have no difficulty negotiating thorns or prickly briars – while, on the other hand, inquisitive badgers or foxes intending to feast on our eggs won't readily stick their sensitive snouts into those kinds of places. And the larger birds who might also steal or break open our eggs for a meal can't penetrate them all that easily either. So, the nest, if well protected, can even be built right on the ground, which we sometimes decide to do in any case.

In this context, the common bramble or blackberry bush, and though perhaps not the most agreeable plant in a pleasant garden setting, is actually ideal for providing protection and seclusion for nesting robins. Not only that, but the shaded density of your typical bramble thicket can be home to hundreds of other tiny creatures. Robins can forage for beetles, bugs and wrigglies of all kinds in there, without having to go very far at all. And then, a little later towards the end of summer the blackberries themselves provide a ready supply of delicious fruit.

Alternatively, an old logpile is also a serviceable place for nesting providing it has an entrance of sorts and a reasonably sized cavity inside with space to build. Whether this is placed in a wooded area, the edge of a path or even against a wall, it really doesn't matter as long as it's well-established and feels 'natural' to us when we investigate. Again, as with the bramble bush, this is the sort of place that furnishes us with a built-in larder of stuff to eat – because all manner of invertebrates just love logpiles too. The only word of caution here is please make sure the whole thing is stable. If necessary support the sides of the pile with posts. That way the logs won't slip or roll and you won't get squashed robins.

One of our favourite places in the past, Mrs Robin and me, was a lovely creeping juniper bush – that variety of juniper that's somewhat spiny in texture and hugs the ground. We could go in and out with food for the babies and the nest was right deep inside on the ground, and nobody could reach it except us. Very nice and cosy. A fine, natural little home it was. And we even came back later in the year for some of the berries.

Anyway, for your information by way of summary, here next is a handy picture indicating some of the most common nesting sites that robins seek out for themselves and will happily occupy for these few vital weeks of the year around nesting time. There are many more places we might choose, of course, and some of them pretty bizarre. I'll shall enjoy telling you all about those shortly.

Robin's Prime Real Estate
Some places where we like to nest

Old outdoor buildings - sheds, secluded ledges, shelves or hidden corners.

To Let

Horizontal or creeping juniper bush. Two or three together are ideal.

Common bramble (blackberry) bushes. An old pot or kettle hidden inside is great, too.

Ivy - preferably mature and clinging to a wall or tree.

A log pile with hidden spaces inside. Please make sure it is stable.

Places where robins like to nest

Eccentric locations

Robins when nesting can be pretty eccentric, especially when we happen to live close to human habitation because there are just so many interesting alternatives for us to explore. For example, we're certainly not averse to making use of all those ledges or nooks and crannies in some of your old buildings – like a garden shed or garage – places with a handy gap or two in the woodwork to fly through and somewhere discreet to make a nest inside like a flower pot or sieve. We have also been known to nest in letter boxes, old coat pockets, peg bags, hats and discarded kettles; in the folds of an unmade bed and upon the open pages of a church bible; on top of an abandoned barbecue; beneath the bonnet of a sports car and (even more recklessly) inside the engine of a fighter plane.

In bygone times there are yet more extraordinary accounts – such as the robin who made her nest in the mast of Nelson's HMS Victory, making use of a cavity made by canon fire – the same mast that Nelson was leaning against when he was mortally wounded at the battle of Trafalgar. Robins do love a hero.

There is even a report of a nest within the structure of a horse-drawn wagon. When the wagon was driven off on what was to be a 100-mile round trip, the parent robin was observed to accompany it, intermittently breaking away to forage for food for its chicks until the wagon was safely returned to its starting place.

Nor are robins at all squeamish about the ambience of their nesting sites. There is a recorded instance from the past of a robin nesting in the skull of an executed criminal whose body had been hung in chains for some years. That's a bit gruesome, isn't it? And there's even a record of a nest being made within the body of a dead cat (I don't mind *that* story quite so much).

The main concern for nesting, wherever it happens, is that it has to be located somewhere we don't expect to be disturbed or messed about with. If we suspect people or animals have discovered our nesting place, we're inclined to get nervous. We might abandon it altogether then and just start a new nest somewhere else. That sounds a bit drastic, I know, but it makes sense when you think about it. We only get a couple of chances each year to get things right when it comes to raising a family. Considerable time and energy will be invested. The female robin will spend days building her nest and will be sitting on the eggs for two weeks. The chicks that hatch from them will remain in the nest for an additional two weeks, moreover, before leaving. So why risk expending all that time and energy in some place that might already be compromised? We just go away and seek out an alternative. And we won't return.

So no matter how curious you might become seeing us carrying nesting material into some hidden nook in your garden, please don't interfere. Don't be a nosy landlord and get too close; don't peer in or otherwise play about with our nesting places. And of course it goes without saying that if we have ventured inside a building via a certain entrance, do make sure you don't go closing it up and shutting us inside by mistake. Take care of these concerns, and you will have a couple of happy robins as neighbours who will gladly make their home alongside yours and raise their family there.

Construction of a robin's nest

Our nest itself is a fine piece of work. About five or six inches in diameter, it's compiled of various layers, beginning with the coarsest and most supportive material at the bottom and finishing with the finest and most comfy at the top. Old dried leaves come first, therefore, for stability and to lay down a good foundation, with a quantity of coarse straw incorporated and even some odd fragments of litter that Mrs Robin might take a fancy to such as paper or card. Then she will gather lots of soft material like moss to build up more height and to form the round bowl-like cradle of the nest itself. She'll turn round and round on top of this from time to time, firming down the shape so it's slightly springy and easy for the eggs to rest in safely and that when it comes to incubation she can sit comfortably on top of it all for lengthy periods.

Finally, she weaves a delicate lining of hair or scraps of wool within the nesting hollow. All this keeps everything well insulated and snug. And because the whole thing is an organic structure it produces a subtle warmth all of its own too. A bit like the material decomposing in a compost heap, only on a much smaller scale, of course (no steam rising out of Mrs Robin's nest has ever been detected). To summarise, here's a bird's-eye view of a typical creation so you can see just what I mean:

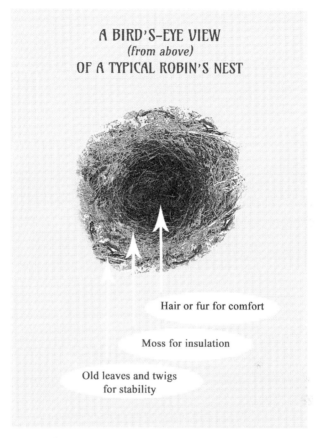

A BIRD'S-EYE VIEW
(from above)
OF A TYPICAL ROBIN'S NEST

Hair or fur for comfort

Moss for insulation

Old leaves and twigs
for stability

Construction of a typical robin's nest

Nesting Boxes

I've described a conventional robin's nest in some detail now. But there's also a good few alternatives lately for us more-domesticated garden robins because we often come across ready-made homes to nest in – what people call 'bird boxes' or 'nesting boxes' – those items you can buy from shops and garden centres. They come in all shapes and sizes, and that's for a good reason most of the time, since different species of birds have different needs when it comes to making a nest inside a box. I mean, the whole thing is a bit odd anyway when you come to think of it. Not exactly natural. But we don't mind, and in fact a well-placed and suitable nestbox is a very attractive proposition for a robin. Only you need to get it right. Here are some handy tips on providing the best sort of home, albeit a temporary one, for Family Robin.

Firstly, we don't approve of those boxes with tiny holes in the front. Those are for birds that are even smaller than we are, like tits. Robins can't squeeze through that sort of tiny aperture, usually only around an inch in size.

We also definitely don't want anything fancy – that is, any item that draws attention to itself and therefore to where we are. No bright colours, plastic or ornamentation therefore, which in my view would be in really bad taste anyway for a classy robin like me. And no wood that has been painted or varnished recently either, or treated with smelly chemicals.

Right ... so now you know what robins don't want. What about something suitable that we *do*? Starting with the top, the ideal box should have a sloping roof to let the rainwater drain off and keep it dry inside. To be fair, most boxes, even the cheapest ones, do have that. But if it is hinged for access, do make sure it can be fastened securely as well to prevent inquisitive squirrels venturing in. Turning next to the entrance: a generous open space at the upper front of the box is what we always look for and expect. The aperture can be as wide as the box itself or a little smaller – like a window frame. But no smaller than four inches, please.

Beneath this opening, we like a good depth to the box. This is so we can build up that supportive foundation to our nesting material that I described earlier, and with a nice soft layer or two on top of that. The top of the bedding has to be low enough for the occupants to be sheltered from the wind if they nestle down, but also high enough so that the baby robins can raise their heads and be fed from the edge, which we perch on when bringing them food. So quite a generous depth is required – say, a couple of inches. Get that right, and the robin building the nest will take care of everything else and ensure the contents fit perfectly inside.

Finally, at the base of the box, and especially if you're in an environment that has frequent rainfall, you might also want to ensure there is a drainage hole – like in a flower pot, only much smaller – just to make sure the whole thing does not become soggy or flooded. If still in any doubt, here's a handy reminder of what's good and not so good in the world of nest-box design:

Nest Boxes for Robins
The good and the bad

No - we don't want round holes, thank you.

Em ... this looks like a bit of a squeeze.

Are you kidding?

Excellent! This really is just about perfect.

Good and bad nesting boxes

If you're a capable DIY person who's handy with wood and things, you can probably see how easy it might be to knock up one yourself. Any old timber will do for structure, as long as it's of a good thickness (say around half an inch or more) – though really, commercially made boxes are so reasonable these days in cost that it's hardly worth going to all that trouble – unless you really want to, that is. The main thing is that it is robin friendly as seen lower-right in the picture, and perhaps equally as important that it is properly located. The greatest bird box in the world is useless if it's not placed in a suitable position. I will come to this next.

Locating the box safely

If, as we have seen, it's advisable to get the shape of the nesting box just right for attracting robins to your garden, then locating it correctly is also a hugely significant factor if you wish to see it inhabited. This is especially true in terms of aspect and height. Whether it's one you've made yourself or one you have bought from a shop or garden centre, you will need to find a sensible place to hang your nesting box.

Firstly, you need to make sure it's secure; that it won't wobble about in the wind and, most importantly of all, that it is in a discreet location that cannot easily be discovered by predators – those wicked cats or unscrupulous magpies.

Also, do please make sure it is not in direct sunlight. It can get pretty uncomfortable for us otherwise, especially during a hot sunny spell, and the chicks don't like that at all. It's preferable, therefore, to secure the back of the box to a north-facing or east-facing wall within a cool, shady surrounding of some kind such as a leafy shrub or climber. A good spread of ivy or honeysuckle for example will do nicely – as long as it's already been growing there for a while and looks and feels established and natural.

Finally, the height at which the box is placed is also fairly critical. To be secure from land-roaming predators it should ideally be between five and six feet from the ground – say, at least shoulder height for an adult.

Perils and Predators of the Robin Nest

The matter of concealment, touched on briefly already, is so important, in fact crucial for us nesting robins, that I am going to go into it in more detail. Different landscapes and areas of countryside have different challenges in this respect. For instance, most urban gardens will inevitably suffer from a domestic cat problem. This is serious. Here in the UK it is estimated that as many as 27 million birds are dispatched by cats annually, and among those, believe you me, there's an awfully high proportion of robins.

Countryside or towns close to the sea could have an additional problem from marauding gulls, while areas close to heathland or chalk downland could suffer from snakes. Many rural areas have populations of badgers and foxes, which are a real menace – while just about everywhere in the UK there are major challenges for robins in the shape of other birds, much bigger birds like magpies, jays, crows or jackdaws. They will jump onto our nest when we're not looking and eat our eggs. And that can be very traumatic.

There are other, even-larger winged predators to contend with such as kestrels, sparrowhawks and buzzards. These are monstrous birds that can hover or circle about in the sky for ages, watching and biding their time before swooping down for a tasty egg or two. If the mood and opportunity arises, they will simply destroy a robins' nest, devouring the contents or even carrying the babies away to serve as a meal for their own young.

And as for those cuckoos I mentioned earlier ... well, I don't even want to think about those dreadful, ghastly things that lay their eggs within other birds' nests and then expect the resident parents to feed and rear them. The young hatchling cuckoo as it grows in vigour (and it's a big strong bird) will even kick out the other resident chicks – which then die – so all that remains is one great cuckoo mouth to feed and two very confused parents. Disgraceful!

The upshot of this horrific litany of crimes against robin eggs is that any practical assistance you can provide is gratefully received. And in respect of those nest boxes, it's never a bad idea to organise a little extra protection for us by constructing a simple surround of wire or plastic mesh. This really will make a difference.

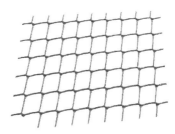

Make sure the gaps are large enough for robins to pass through, but not so large that the bigger birds or squirrels are able to squeeze in after us. Two-inch plastic mesh fencing is ideal. You'll need to make sure the box is covered at the top and sides as well as the front – so cut out three or four pieces and weave them together with a little bit of string or garden wire. That'll do the trick and will keep our chicks safe, especially at those moments when we are away foraging for food – because, like I say, that's when those bigger predatory birds will choose to strike. Secure the mesh at a distance of at least a couple of inches from the opening of the box itself, and that way they won't be able to stretch their horrid beaks through even if they try. Finally, for the ultimate in security for the robin family, do please encourage plenty of foliage to grow over it all so everything is camouflaged.

The very best nest box I ever had was one just like the final example in our illustration earlier, secured firmly to a wall about six feet from the ground. It was encased in a splendid wire-mesh surround, set a couple of inches from the box itself and had obviously been put up a good few months earlier by the gardener chap because the whole lot was already covered in a lush canopy of beautiful green ivy. Marvellous. Top man. Deserves the Nobel Prize for services to robins, in my opinion.

Cleaning the box

This is probably a good place to tell you about how to clean and maintain the nest box – important because at the end of the nesting season, after a batch of robins has been successfully reared, the bedding will be pretty grubby and could even be smelly enough to attract predators. It can also have mites or fleas, which will lie in readiness for any new occupants – which is why it is rarely visited again by adult robins. Thus, at the end of the nesting season, it is important to take down the box once you are absolutely certain it is no longer in use and extract the old nest (you might want to wear gloves and a protective mask for this job). Dispose of all the waste nesting material (always suitable for composting, by the way), before cleaning inside thoroughly with a disinfectant wipe. Then remove any residue smells from the disinfectant with a clean, damp cloth before allowing everything to dry thoroughly – hopefully in readiness for the next season.

Robins' eggs

So, once they have been laid, what exactly are robins' eggs like? Well, they are tiny, as you would expect coming from small birds like us – only a little over three-quarters of an inch (20mm) in length. Once she has finished building her nest, Mrs Robin will be laying one of these each day, usually in the mornings, until she feels she has done enough. The growing process within the eggs is then stimulated and encouraged by the warmth of Mrs Robin sitting gently on top of them, the process of incubation.

The number of eggs – the 'clutch, as it is called' - varies according to geography and seasonal factors, but typically consists of between four and six eggs of up to about 2.7g each in weight. Curiously, the eggs actually diminish in weight as the incubation period proceeds – coming in at around just 2.4g a couple of weeks later and shortly before hatching occurs. This is due to moisture from inside gradually escaping through the partly porous shell as the embryo grows within. The shell material is peppered with numerous microscopic holes through which this moisture escapes.

The eggs themselves are of an attractive off-white hue, not particularly shiny and with a delicate surface patination of fine reddish-brown speckles. Also, like many an egg, the shape is clearly more rounded or 'blunter' at one end than the other, and it is here where the patination often appears the more concentrated.

Mrs Robin has to be incredibly patient during this period, keeping still for lengthy periods and only occasionally leaving the nest by day, while also having to remain there all night. By the way, remember that special brood patch on the abdomen I told you about earlier? Now is when it comes in handy. This is because, should the eggs ever get cold, they will cease to support a live chick within, and all will be lost. If the nest is in the open, she will also have to sit with her wings spread over the little ones as they hatch to keep them dry. A rainy day is not much fun for a naked new-born robin, which is why we often venture into sheltered places like sheds or those splendid nest boxes of yours to make our nests.

Robin duties

As you can imagine, what with all this sitting around for hours, Mrs Robin will have become pretty hungry by the time she does finally have an opportunity to leave the nest – which she will want to do at least every hour or so. And though she will grab a bite to eat for herself soon enough, I am also expected to be on hand to feed her. I usually am. But if I happen to be otherwise occupied – with the important business of singing, for instance – she will soon discover my whereabouts and give me a nudge to remind me of my duties (actually a little bit more than just a 'nudge' sometimes). But it doesn't matter. We both enjoy these little rituals. It reminds us that we are an *item*, with a shared purpose.

Hatching out

Meanwhile, back at the nest and deep within the protective shell of the eggs the tiny robins-to-be are steadily growing and increasing in size by absorbing the nutrients already present within the shell: the egg white and the yolk.

As for obtaining oxygen inside, which every embryo requires of course, this is also taken care of because a certain amount of air is already trapped within the shell from when it was formed, while fresh air can also enter through those microscopic holes in its surface in the same way as moisture can escape. So the little chick-to-be inside can breathe perfectly well all the while it's growing.

And how very fast it does grow! Over the short two-week incubation period its shape alters rapidly, developing from a tiny speck into a feisty little critter sufficiently robust to peck its way out of its shell from within. In this endeavour, it makes use of a special pointy spur on its beak that has evolved precisely for this purpose, bashing away until the shell is punctured and it manages to thrust its head through and clamber out. Can you imagine how much energy and determination that requires from such a little creature?

Hooray – the chick is born! And we just love it when this happens.

Hatchling (with another on the way)

What baby robins eat, and when

Strange, those baby robins once they hatch from the eggs – they are so very small we can hardly get anything into their tiny beaks at all. I suppose you would probably think of them, the hatchlings, as being quite bizarre little things at first, rather like little strips of red meat with beaks. But to us they're gorgeous. Like little miracles.

Luckily at this time of the year, just when we really need it, the menu for robins becomes far more extensive and varied. A whole range of new creatures including caterpillars flies and spiders suddenly becomes available after the grim shortages of winter. And that's just great because at the moment tiny items like these are ideal for those nestlings of ours.

Right at the start however, the chicks can't take solid food at all – not for a day or two. And so at this delicate stage we sustain them by gathering and regurgitating a partly digested mixture of flies and tiny bugs that we store in our stomachs or throats. That might sound a bit gross to a refined sort of human with impeccable table manners (you *do* have impeccable table manners, don't you?) but because birds don't have teeth, we have to break up our food inside – making use of a part of the digestive tract called the gizzard, a powerful organ that grinds everything down with the aid of digestive chemicals and sometimes even small pieces of grit that we ingest to help the process along. When rearing young, therefore, especially when they are newly hatched, we can bring up food at just the right consistency to slide down into those little beaks. A bit like what you would call a liquid feed only a bit more lumpy.

A few days later and we can give them the first proper solid food: those flies and tiny bugs I mentioned just now, for which they really are so grateful. So off we go straight away to find some more. The more we feed them, the bigger and more hungry they get, until just the sight of those gaping throats when we return to the nest each time is enough to send us wild.

Feeding Frenzy

The young ones grow fast. And after about four days from hatching, they are ready to take slightly larger fragments of food – like whole flies or spiders. But we can also chomp up an earthworm or two for them now, and just about manage to place the pieces into their mouths – until pretty soon, into the second week from hatching, we can already begin to fetch much larger items for them – like whole beetles or grubs, and they just love these. They seem to want more and more now – insatiable. Though to be fair, when you consider that after just two short weeks from hatching they will be aiming to reach the same size and weight as their parents, it really isn't that surprising. That's a lot of growing to be done in such a short space of time.

The Hungry Robin

MENU

SPRING SEASONAL FARE

Earthworms
Beetles & Bugs
Caterpillars (subject to availability)
Spiders (limited selection)
Centipedes & Millipedes
Flies

VEGETARIAN

~~Berries (wild)~~
~~Hedgerow Fruits~~
Plant and weed seeds (various)

DESSERT

Specialities fresh from the bird table

Bread and biscuit crumbs
Finely choped or grated cheese rind
Mealworms

Opening times: sunrise to sunset daily.
Garden Lane, Wrigglesbury, Hunts, AR0 8IN

Spring season's menu at The Hungry Robin

Yes, an abundance of lovely nibbles for us robins to savour now as proper *live* food becomes more and more in demand as the chicks grow. But we don't trouble ourselves about all this extra work. As long as we can both stay fit and well, it really is great fun and we soon begin to realise that we are pretty much hooked on the idea of hunting and taking food to those little nestlings of ours. It becomes a kind of feeding frenzy, with most of what we gather going to them: very little to ourselves. And although I like to think I go about the process in a reasonably calm and measured way, some robins go berserk.

That's when you'll see us, Mrs Robin and me, coming and going constantly to and from the nest with great beakfuls of food, often one of us flying in just as the other shoots out – and always heading off in different directions. It's nothing for us to visit the nest like this as often as every three or four minutes now, and we dash around so fast that you'd think there must be at least a half-dozen of us out there. I swear I even met myself the other day coming out from the nest box, it was all so frantic.

Appearance of nestlings

As you can see from the illustration earlier, when they first hatch, the little ones are more or less naked, very tiny – and also completely blind. Their bodies are almost transparent too, and you can even see their organs and their little hearts beating away inside. And although they can sense our presence through movement – like when we bounce about when returning to the nest with food, they aren't able to see us until after about four or five days from hatching. It's also around this time that they become aware of the sounds we make and learn to recognise our voices. That's important, because eventually we will be calling them from outside and encouraging them to leave the nest when they are ready. Though that's a good few days away yet.

Naturally, at this time, their feathers grow fast. Although they are only downy feathers at first, quite fluffy in appearance, at least they help keep their bodies warm when Mrs Robin is away from the nest. But soon the babes will grow proper feathers like ours, which start out as a collection of tiny straw-like sheaths on their skin. Quickly, these sheaves fall away to reveal the maturing feathers within, and these will develop rapidly so as to cover the whole body and face while the chick is still in the nest.

Their earlier bulgy-eyed appearance diminishes towards the end of this process too, so that they start to look more like proper little birds. And by this stage, having also become large enough to keep each other warm, they will be left alone to huddle together at night, while Mrs Robin roosts somewhere nearby. She has to do this anyway during the final days of the nesting period otherwise there just wouldn't be enough room for everyone inside.

Hungry nestling chicks with ivy

Nature red in tooth and claw

The nest is meant to be a safe place for the little ones. But the natural world outside where robins dwell can be a pretty gruesome and frightening place. Everything is competing constantly for resources, you see, while also desperately trying to protect and rear its own offspring. I believe it was a famous Victorian painter chap who once described it as 'nature red in tooth and claw' and that just about sums it up for us robins right now because we are certainly no exception.

In other words, it really is carnage out here. And when we are on the hunt, nothing that moves is safe ... well, unless it's bigger than a robin, that is. We become a bit more cautious then because we don't want to get eaten ourselves. That would only mean our young ones would starve, and that would never do. So we take care always and keep an eye open for any unpleasant creatures that might be looking to prey on us.

That's why you will often see me looking up to the sky, because there are some pretty ferocious birds at large up there – like all those horrid sparrowhawks, kestrels or buzzards that I mentioned earlier. And they are bigger, *much bigger* than us. Giants, they are and you definitely wouldn't want to mess with them. They are, in fact, a significant problem for robins all through the spring and summer months, and I shall elaborate a little more on this topic in the next chapter. But for now, it's back to the story of that rapidly growing family of ours.

Etiquette and hygiene within the nest

The nestlings are remarkably clever really, and they seem to have an instinctive understanding almost from the start of just how important it is to keep still and quiet while we are away from them and searching for their food – an etiquette of survival they're born with. When they notice us returning they do get a bit excited all of a sudden and so do we when we realise we must satisfy their hunger as quickly as possible. It's quite a rush at times, but we do try our best to make sure all the chicks have an equal share.

We *try*, yes – but there is always one rascal, usually the first one to have hatched, who will demand more than its fair share. It's hard to concentrate on feeding the others when the big greedy one at the front is so insistent. But that's the lust for life, I suppose: to want to grow and be nourished. And you can bet your life this will also be the very same chick at the front of the queue wanting to leave the nest ahead of all the others in a week or so's time. The process of 'fledging' as it is called.

Meanwhile, the nest itself has to be kept in an hygienic state. The egg shells, once broken and discarded, are promptly removed by the parents and taken off some distance, with the female occasionally eating some of the fragments herself – thus recycling their vital minerals. But hygiene in the nest also means being careful with the food we bring in. Inevitably, some of it gets dropped and abandoned, and if you examine a robin's nest after it's vacated you will often notice little morsels of food at the very bottom. These are items that for one reason or another the hatchlings were unable to get down or were dropped during the feeding procedure. The babies will not eat anything that does not come directly from its parents, and anything dropped into the bacteria-rich base of a nest will naturally be ignored. Another valuable survival trait.

Poo – the routine of the faecal sac

But what about baby-robin waste? What happens to all that digested foodstuff when it comes out the other end? Well, our little robins have a brilliant way of parcelling up their poo in what is called a *faecal sac*. These are pale little packages within a thin but strong mucus membrane that we can grasp gently in our beaks and carry off – usually to a good remote distance so as not to advertise the nest's location. The faecal sac routine also avoids any unpleasant odours becoming caught up in the nest that could attract certain predators.

Fortunately, not all the chicks do one at the same time (which could prove somewhat overwhelming, to say the least), but rather the chick among the brood that is currently receiving food will simply raise the other end when it's finished and eject the sac for us to pick up – a bit like a nappy in a bag, and I'm glad to report that it rarely bursts. We quickly get used to the whole procedure – though sometimes I like to head off to the birdbath afterwards to wash my face. The chicks do begin to look lovely by this stage, anyway, so it's worth it.

I mean, just look at this little fellow!

Junior

This one's got my-shaped beak too, don't you think? And you can definitely see Mrs Robin's eyes there when it glances up. Well ... perhaps not everyone would notice that, but I'm sure you'll agree our babies are just beautiful, aren't they?

They really are ... aren't they?

Oh, please yourself.

When the young ones leave the nest

After a couple of weeks from hatching, anytime between 12 and 14 days to be more specific, the youngsters will have left the nest – or 'fledged' as it is properly termed. Inevitably there simply comes a time when they are too restless and inquisitive to keep in one place any longer and – like I say – there's always one troublemaker at the head of the queue who's first to tumble out ahead of all the others and hop around for the first time. Then it really is 'action stations' and everything suddenly becomes very frantic indeed because the others will soon want to follow suit.

It could take another day before the youngest of the bunch, the 'runt' of the brood as it's sometimes rather unkindly called, will finally pluck up courage and leave, but a special call from me or Mrs Robin, whose voice it recognises well now, is sufficient motivation eventually and within a very short period they will all be out and away. You might just see one of us adults pop in later to check that the nest is empty, but none of the babes will return. And that is the end of the nesting period. An amazingly busy and exhausting four or five weeks.

The growing is not over yet though. Far from it, and there continue to be some pretty dramatic alterations in appearances still to come. Shortly after leaving the nest, fledgling robins are rather dull little birds with a brown speckled plumage. They don't have any indication of that magnificent red breast yet, and their faces still seem to be all mouth and beak, especially when awaiting food – which continues to be more often than not, I must say.

They still can't feed themselves, you see, even now, and they still need to open those big jaws to receive whatever we have to offer, so there's no need for their beaks to be sharp and sensitive, as with adult birds. As the baby robin grows, however, the beak will lose its characteristically flat and grumpy appearance and become sharper and more elongated, and thus suitable for locating and picking up its own food in time.

Summary

Yes, spring really is a breathtaking and utterly frantic season for robins, and it makes me quite exhausted just trying to tell you all about it. By way of summary of all the things we have looked at so far, here is a handy timeline of the nesting occupancy from egg to fledgling.

The Diary of a Robin's Nest

DAYS

Day	
1	
2	
3	A single egg is
4	laid each day.
5	Typically 5 or 6 in all
6	
7	After final egg is laid, the
8	incubation period begins
9	
10	
11	Incubation of eggs
12	continues for around
13	13 or 14 days while
14	each chick grows
15	inside
16	
17	
18	
19	Hatchlings begin to break through
20	their shells, one at a time, and adult
21	robins start to feed regurgitated food
22	to them
23	
24	Adult birds bring small items of solid food.
25	The chicks' eyes have opened
26	
27	
28	Chicks are able to take large
29	items of food brought to the nest
30	
31	They keep on eating, and
32	eating, and eating!
33	
34	
35	First fledgling leaves the nest.
36	Others quickly follow

The nesting timeline, from egg to fledgling

Please note, what you see illustrated here is a rough guide only. There are plenty of variations in timing according to weather conditions; food supply or how many eggs make up the clutch. The main point to take from all this, however, is that it will have been typically all of five weeks from the laying of that first egg until our little ones are all up and away.

Also there is the important matter of fully developing their flight feathers. These are not quite ready yet, and unfortunately it will be a good few days yet before the youngsters can properly take to the wing. I'll explain how all this happens in the next chapter.

So can we relax and take things easy now? No, I'm afraid not - we're not out of the woods yet. With no longer the relative safety and protection of the nest to house our family, we must now face some of the biggest challenges ever as our fledglings begin to encounter so many of those same dangers that we, as adult robins, have had to deal with on a daily basis all our lives – the threat from mischievous cats, from fast-winged hawks; from crafty foxes; wicked rodents and sneaky snakes. Why, overseas in some parts of Europe even the people there can prove lethal, catching us in nets or in traps before eating us. Yes, *people – eating us!* Can you believe it?

No wonder those European robins, whom we meet sometimes when they visit us later in the year, are so much more bashful than those of us in the UK – a land where robins are, I'm glad to say, actually protected by both law and custom.

Yes, it's a tough old world out here for our vulnerable

and naive little fledglings, and in truth only fewer than half the clutch will probably survive the coming weeks and make it through to what is called the juvenile stage – and then with even fewer surviving into proper adulthood later in the year.

That's heartbreaking, when you come to think of it. And I shall tell you all about how we cope with such horrors next as we turn our attentions to the delights of summer.

Robin in Summer

SUMMER

Long days and short nights are what summer is all about – and lots of daylight too by which to get things done. That's just as well, because there really are some major robin–family matters to deal with now, what with having to look out for the youngsters once they've left the nest and to place them discreetly where they are less likely to be seen by unfriendly eyes. A tall order because just about every other creature out here has its own hungry babes to feed, and tiny robins make the ideal takeaway snack.

Robins are not really all that good at counting, which is probably just as well, because from among the four or five fledglings who leave the nest, only a couple will probably still be around in this dangerous world by the time they have learned how to fly properly.

The main problem is that their flight feathers, those on their wings and tail, are still not fully formed and won't be for at least another four or five days. And although they are capable of toddling along on the ground and can even hop or flutter up into bushes, there's still a fair way to go in respect of being able to take to the air easily. Thus, the journey they embark upon now away from the nest is one of peril and hidden danger.

Summer is naturally a time of amazing growth and abundance. The canopies of leaves above, the grasses and tangled stems of ferns and bracken below – they are all far more extensive now compared to even just a few weeks ago. It's all very lovely, mysterious and tempting – and buzzing with a rich source of food for our growing family. But all this lush summer greenery is a mixed blessing for us robins because it can also harbour all manner of dangerous creatures that are unkind to birds. I mean, you just don't know what's lurking there when you dive down into the thick of it in search of a tasty morsel – for you might just end up as a tasty morsel yourself if there's a sneaky cat or fox in hiding.

We have to be extra vigilant in other words while also watching over our youngsters and making sure they continue to get all the nourishment they need until they can fully recognise these dangers and fend for themselves.

One of the cleverest ways we go about this is through a number of well-rehearsed calls and signals that we share between us whenever we sense that trouble might be about. And because we also have to set an example to the youngsters regarding how to sing anyway at this time, it's a bit like music school for robins out here at the moment.

The special calls that robins make

For a young fledgling to be exposed to a good vocalist is

important and usually makes a difference as to how well they will sing later into adulthood. That's why, apart from my usual broad repertoire of spectacular and technically accomplished vocal performances during winter and spring, there has to be this one final little flurry of song to be delivered at the start of summer once the young have vacated the nest. This is to teach the youngsters how to sing and to assert themselves, with father as teacher. Knowing they are listening, I demonstrate my unique vocal style and show them all the moves that go with it – a sort of robin equivalent of *Dad dancing*. I'm sure they're impressed, and one day they will thank me.

But it's not just about singing and passing on our vocal skills to others. A responsible parent like me with a growing family to look after will also have a few additional sounds up his sleeve – short warning messages or calls to action that are made between male and female partners or between parents and fledglings that prove especially useful at present out here in the wild and unpredictable world.

Firstly, there is a distinct, high-pitched 'tick, tick' noise that we emit if any of us spot a predator on the ground – typically a cat or even a person like you who, even though of no evil intent, I'm sure, might well be getting too close for comfort. Sorry, but we just can't take any chances, you see.

Then there is a similar albeit slightly more drawn-out alarm call of a 'tseep, tseep' kind of sound indicating the appearance of predators on the wing, like hawks or kestrels. These calls are especially urgent and are not to be ignored. They help ensure that not just my family but all robins in the vicinity stay safe. I used that on a regular basis when Mrs Robin was sitting on the nest to alert her whenever anything suspicious was approaching overhead and she could then always lay low.

Meanwhile, the fledgling robins have their own distinct call – one directed at their parents – namely the begging call for food. Even though they can forage a little for themselves after just a few days, they will be expecting to receive more substantial items from us for a good few weeks yet to come. They still always seem to be peckish, and we do still like to provide them with little treats whenever we can. But first we have to find them – for which they assist us by emitting a chirpy little contact call at intervals, so we almost always have a good idea of their location. These are usually places we've already guided them to anyway and where we expect them to remain sequestered.

That's a nice sound, and we don't mind that at all. But anything else and we are immediately on alert and watchful. We have to be. Only the most switched-on of parents will ever rear a successful brood, and it really is a constant challenge keeping them out of harm's way, and keeping us alive too for them.

Fledglings at large – please don't touch

During these first few days after departing the nest, which as we have seen takes place when the youngsters are around 13 or 14 days old, the young robins are wonderfully docile and obedient. Being dependent still on their parents, they can easily be encouraged to follow us around, which helps us to hide them, preferably in thick undergrowth or bushes where predators cannot easily detect their presence. All we need to do is let out a little *cheep* to get them to obey, and they will normally stay put when we leave them, keeping silent until we come back to check how they're doing.

If you chance upon a baby robin you will recognise it by its brown, motley plumage, short tail and a rather comical-shaped beak. The thing is, please don't conclude that it is an orphan or abandoned youngster just because it is sitting there on its own. The odds are very slim indeed that it is really unattended. The parent robins will be aware of it, and although we might be some distance away, we will be returning to feed it regularly.

In other words, do not rescue it! It does not need rescuing. It can be very frightening for a little robin to be picked up by clumsy hands. And curious or well-intentioned people can do damage by meddling in this way.

Don't worry! The little robin really is OK. It just needs leaving alone. Thanks.

Nasty things that eat robins

Sadly, any robin who gives the matter a little consideration will have to face up to the harsh reality that most of us won't have the luxury of dying quietly in old age but will probably meet a sticky end one way or another. There are no hospitals for robins when we become injured or sick; no care homes when we grow old and infirm. We just have to accept that we are part of the food chain, and will eventually be consumed by something or the other. Even at night they're after us. And every time we go to sleep we never really know whether we will wake up the next day in one piece.

As I mentioned earlier, most of our enemies out here will have new-born families of their own to feed, so their behaviour is almost forgivable in an odd sort of way – while robins, for their part, certainly do their fair share of devouring other creatures too. But killing dear little robins, barely out of the nest and who haven't even had a chance to grow up and enjoy themselves ... well, that's really bad form in my opinion.

I've already told you about those birds that raid our nests and eat our eggs, but as the following illustration reveals, a few naughty magpies are the least of our worries. Just take a look at this rogues' gallery and you'll see what I mean. Being a robin really does mean living life on the edge. It's incredibly dangerous, and we can't do an awful lot about it.

Robins' Predators

Buzzards - with up to a four-foot wingspan, these giants circle overhead before swooping to kill.

Sparrowhawks - relying on the element of surprise, they fly at blistering speed.

Kestrels - these sky-hovering monsters have amazing eyesight, sharp talons and powerful beaks.

Owls - at dawn or dusk, they will swoop silently on small birds, especially when food is scarce.

Corvids (magpies, jays, crows) - fierce woodland predators that eat our eggs and hatchlings.

Foxes - opportunists that eat eggs and set their powerful jaws into vulnerable young fledglings.

Badgers - great lumbering, sharp-clawed creatures who will eat our eggs and even our nestlings.

Squirrels - might look cute, but they raid nests, take our eggs and will even eat the hatchlings.

Stoats and Weasels - sinuous, quick-moving creatures that can squeeze in just about anywhere.

Hedgehogs - these prickly creatures will waddle into a nest and devour our eggs.

Snakes. - though a little too slow to catch adult birds, they are very partial to our eggs.

Rodents - rats and mice will raid our nests and take the eggs when we might not be watching.

Domestic Cats - pampered monsters that creep up on us and then pounce and kill just for amusement!

Predators – the major culprits

Quite a formidable catalogue of horrors, isn't it? And by no means an exhaustive list. If you are a robin living near the sea for instance, you can be sure the gulls there won't be doing you any favours either.

The menace from above is an ever-present problem, and that's why you'll often notice me cocking my head inquisitively to one side, glancing up at the sky. It's a useful habit to cultivate, I can assure you, because it's not unknown for an adult robin like me to be picked off by a rapacious sparrowhawk. These terrifying birds are so fast on the wing. They can reach speeds of 30 mph, so you just don't have a chance of avoiding them if they decide to come at you, which is almost always when you're unawares. The kestrel is a bit like that too, and though perhaps not as fast, it's another creature that views a small garden bird, especially a young juvenile robin, as fair game for their young.

Likewise with those wretched great buzzards – huge birds with a wingspan of up to four feet. Can you imagine how enormous that looks to a tiny robin? The survival of their own offspring is paramount for them too, of course, just as it is for us. No quarter given.

The only saving grace is that buzzards are cumbersome and ponderous enough that you definitely know when they're about. Very affected birds really, they circle round and round in the air for hours showing off and making eerie noises, so we know when to keep low and out of sight when we hear them.

Unlikely allies

Yes, it's all pretty tense and unforgiving out here in the wild right now – though I'm glad to say we are not entirely without allies. Gardeners sometimes keep a look out for us, while relief and protection can also arrive from some unexpected quarters. A pleasant surprise occasionally is to discover that the crows are actually making themselves useful for once because they too need to protect their eggs and their young, and so they chase the buzzards and kestrels away. There's nothing I enjoy as much as observing a good 'dog fight' in the sky among them – even better when the jackdaws join in.

On the ground, meanwhile, you can see from our illustration that there are just as many things to watch out for in the shape of rodents, snakes, foxes and badgers. But again, this all depends on where we live and on local conditions and environment.

In truth, I suppose badgers aren't a huge problem, being nocturnal creatures and only hunting at night when all our baby robins are placed somewhere secure. You would have to be really unlucky as a robin to be picked off by a lumbering badger. But we still don't like them because they eat so many of the nutritious things that robins rely on, like earthworms. Your typical adult badger will eat hundreds of these in a night. Isn't that greedy? And then we're obliged to wake up in the morning after all that and try to find our breakfast!

Cats

Now we come to a very delicate subject indeed: domestic cats. I don't like them at all. From a robin's perspective they are really sneaky and wicked. A cat will pursue us just out of curiosity; for fun or for sport. How disgraceful! These pampered house pets don't normally have the excuse of having young of their own to look after, and they are rarely in want of food themselves. Worse, when a cat hides up and stalks and pounces on our little ones it doesn't even seem to get around to actually eating them. Apparently this is because cats don't much like the taste of robins and won't generally swallow robin flesh. But they do still take it upon themselves to kill robins, and often cruelly.

That's why if I spot one lurking in the garden I emit one of those sharp 'tick, tick' sounds that I described earlier, which warns the young ones to lie low. Mrs Robin will do likewise. But unfortunately by the time they have heard this it's often too late. If you include our feline friends in any listing of all the different ways that robins can die – from hawks or mousetraps to drowning; from fighting with other robins to flying headlong into windows or being hit by cars – the violent leanings of the domestic cat is by far the leading cause.

Yes, we know they're your pets – some of you reading this – and we know you love them, but wouldn't it be a good idea if you could provide the little dears with something like, say, a bell collar so we can at least hear them creeping up on us? These are items that really don't cost much; they come in all kinds of fancy colours and styles and there is no evidence that the bell causes any distress to the pussycat itself.

Every pet owner has to arrive at their own decision in this respect, of course. The collar must be properly fitted and should have a 'quick release' mechanism in case the animal becomes snagged up. But studies indicate that a collar and bell of this kind can reduce bird mortality from cats by upwards of 40%. And that's definitely something worth considering I reckon.

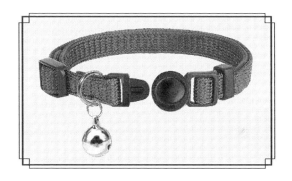

Bell & collar: a lifesaver for robins everywhere

It's all very unfair if you ask me. Songbirds like robins spend hours feeding and fattening up our little ones only for them to be hunted down by some idle, knavish creature. They'll be sorry, all our enemies, that's for sure, if they wake up one day and we're all gone – because who will fill the garden with good joyful singing then, eh? You can hardly say those crows and magpies are much use in the musical department. A badger just grunts and snorts its way through life. And we all know what a cat or fox sounds like when it opens its mouth, if it opens it at all – *dreadful*.

Anyway, apart from all that I suppose there's really not all that much to worry about. The main point to take away from all this is you have to be brave to be a robin. Courage is not an optional extra. And in any case there are lots more important things to be getting on with right now – namely savouring the joys of watching those cute youngsters of ours steadily changing from clumsy juveniles into proper handsome, red-breasted adults later in the year. That really is a great joy and satisfaction. In fact, Mrs Robin and I agree it's such a pleasure, that it begs the question: should we maybe try for another lot this year and do it all over again?

Another brood?

As I mentioned before, there are no hard and fast rules when it comes to the 'timeline' of breeding – not in the realm of bird life. Our cousins the blackbirds and thrushes might already have been busy with their second brood for quite some time now, in and out of their nests constantly with all the comings and goings of anxious parents.

Like us, they can get started very early in the year, as early as February or March following a mild winter, and then they will have another brood later on in the spring. Most pairs of robins will have at least two as well, and a third cannot be ruled out in the middle of the summer, especially if the weather is favourable and there seems likely to be a good supply of food ahead. It does happen –

and, honestly, some robins just don't know when to stop. Some have even been known to feed the young of other robin families. Some, even the young of another species of bird!

In this context, it's worth bearing in mind that if a third brood is started, the first and second will still require attention for a good few weeks yet. So while the female is away sitting on yet another nestful of eggs the male will still be having to feed the young from earlier batches – flying about frantically with beakfuls of food before rushing off to wherever the fledglings are waiting. The first batch will probably be roaming all over the place by this time too. It's hard work. And though a third endeavour is not impossible, generally speaking the later in the year a nest is active the less likely it is to result in a wholly successful outcome.

To be honest we've usually all had enough by now anyway. Thus, the glorious summer months are rightly taken up with the important business of looking after those we've already brought into the world and enjoying our time with them. We still have a lot to teach them, anyway. They learn fast – they have to. And so with any luck there will still be more than enough hungry mouths to keep us busy for quite some time to come.

And you know what? We love every minute of it.

Young robin feeding from adult

Summer: an abundance of food

Summer is not solely about family concerns, of course. Life goes on in other ways, and these long lazy days ensure plenty of leisure time and a tantalising variety of food to savour.

Indeed, as you can see from the robins' menu for summer, we really are rather spoilt for choice at this time of the year. The whole world seems to be buzzing with delicious little morsels; the hedges and undergrowth teeming with all kinds of exotic delicacies, from juicy worms and centipedes to dainty aphids, crunchy beetles and wriggly spiders of all kinds. Yes, a robin gets to appreciate a distinctly finer pallet in the summer months as opposed to those desperate days of winter when frankly to survive at all we're often obliged to eat just about anything that's going. It's a time of the year that provides a great opportunity for culinary exploration, in other words, and there's not a lot we won't try at least once out of curiosity.

There are some notable exceptions though. Slugs - they taste just awful, don't they? And then there's also those butterflies. We rarely touch them – or if we do, we soon learn not to. They might look very pretty and colourful but they can sometimes make me feel quite ill if I swallow one. The good news, though, is they lay their eggs on plants and leaves, and these soon hatch and turn into nice juicy caterpillars – though even here, a robin has to exercise caution. We learn.

The Hungry Robin
MENU

SUMMER SEASONAL FARE

Earthworms (limited availability when dry)
Beetles & Bugs
Caterpillars
Spiders - *petit*
Centipedes & Millipedes
Maggots, grubs & larvae
Grasshoppers
Moths

VEGETARIAN

Plant and weed seeds (various)
Early Ripened Fruits

DESSERT

Secialities fresh from the bird table

Peanut Pâté (unsalted)
Wholemeal Crusts gently steeped in spring water

Opening times: sunrise to sunset daily.
Garden Lane, Wrigglesbury, Hunts, AR0 8IN

Summer season's menu at The Hungry Robin

Roaming Robins

As summer progresses, and though we might still feel a bit tired at moments, we become contented robins – and with plenty of time on our hands, even a little inquisitive too. There is a more open and relaxed feel to all the gardens, woods and hedgerows. What with such a super-abundance of food – more than enough to go round – we robins tend not to be so territorial as we once were earlier in the year. You feel you want to roam a little bit now, to explore things. And providing you keep a low profile you can be pretty safe doing so. After all, there really is so much to experience and investigate in the big wide world, and we haven't had a chance to do anything like this for months.

How quickly it all seems to be changing. Summer's vigorous march is relentless and there hardly seems a spare patch of ground that doesn't get covered by some kind of flowering plant or bush. Campion and wild parsley line the hedgerows, and wild honeysuckle and elder too, along with an amazing variety of other shrubs and vines weaving in and out – like those great white trumpets of columbine that you gardeners are always pulling down, only to be replaced by new ones almost overnight. Funny.

I must say, we do prefer the hedges when they are like this, and we rarely need to work too hard to find our food – while beyond these safe enclaves of ours the great fields with their swaying wheat and barley stretch away to an horizon that for us robins is of a quite bewildering distance. These are places where we rarely venture. You only hear those noisy jackdaws or crows out there anyway, calling to one another, their voices harsh – or perhaps more agreeably the sound of a skylark twittering away, ascending higher and higher into the sky. I don't mind those.

Observations on peculiar human activity

What I can't help noticing though at this time of the year, is that there are a lot of people like you outside enjoying yourselves in your gardens. And working hard too sometimes even in the hot weather. Fascinating. And a robin like me naturally becomes curious as to what exactly all this is about. What with mowing the lawns and managing the vegetable patch and all those flowers you have, from dahlias to sweet peas, from geraniums to roses that need so much attention, you do all seem to have a lot on your plate, I must say. (Funny, that saying – about having a lot on your plate, because for robins we can never really have too much on *our* plate. But I digress.)

Gardeners and growers benefit of course from the presence of us robins whether they appreciate it or not because we eat plenty of the things you regard as pests: little wrigglies that are definitely also busy at this time of the year making a great nuisance of themselves – at least from your perspective – multiplying in vast numbers and attacking all the leaves of your plants and vegetables. With our eager beaks we help keep the numbers down. And I suspect this goes part of the way to explaining why we like gardeners so much, and gardeners like us. It's a good arrangement and a nice sort of friendship that has blossomed over the years. The only thing I find puzzling is that in all the time I've been watching you digging away and turning over the soil for hours on end, I've never once seen any of you eat a single worm or spider!

Sometimes, too, we watch you going about your activities and wish we could communicate and let you know how we feel about what you get up to – because, to be frank, you really could do a little better sometimes in making it easier for us to forage for food or to keep safe. Interested? Right, well here's a chance for me to pass on a few handy tips on behalf of robins everywhere, and I shan't let it go to waste.

Constructive changes

If you want to experiment with some new additions or make constructive changes to the layout of your garden, you might consider including some nice fruit-bearing shrubs and hedges – items that will provide additional food supplies for birds during the autumn and winter months. Native species of plants are best for this purpose. Robins haven't got much time for rare, exotic cultivars – or conifers for that matter, especially those wretched leylandii bushes. We much prefer it if you grow native species like elder, ivy or holly – plants that produce an abundance of berries. A notable exception would perhaps be an exotic grapevine against a south-facing wall if it's warm enough. You can find a more complete list of our favoured plants in the next chapter by the way, when many of the fruits themselves become available in autumn.

Meanwhile, I'll confess that the cultivated varieties of berries and soft fruit that you like to grow for the table can also prove very tempting for us robins. You're not the only ones who are partial to strawberries; to ripe red cherries, or lovely sweet currants – we love those too. Trouble is so do most other birds out here, and I suppose that's the reason you keep those splendid fruit bushes of yours under cages or netting – or why you shoo us off when we get too close. It's almost as if you imagine we're going to try and sneak in underneath the netting or examine it for holes and get in when you're not looking. The very idea!

Oh well, never mind. If you could remember to throw out a few of the old damaged fruits occasionally, we'd be chuffed.

Bird Tables and feeding stations

This brings me to a very interesting topic. I've not mentioned bird tables very much so far, or their more modern equivalent 'feeding stations' but these are items that, perversely, some people tend to set up in their gardens during the summer months. I say *perversely* because it's at just this time of the year when we need them the least – nor do we require the sheer extravagance of foods arrayed on them in such profusion. Nuts, fat-balls, seeds, mealworms – such a variety, that you will inevitably attract a variety of birds too, and a veritable orgy of feeding ensues. But that can be a mixed blessing. The adage of 'If some is good, more is not necessarily better' certainly holds true here.

After all, who wants all those other greedy birds hanging around? Not us robins, that's for sure. Apart from the social bonds we form with our own partners and offspring we are fastidious and solitary creatures by default, not at all gregarious like, say, finches or sparrows. In other words we hate crowds. And by the way, we aren't particularly wild about commercially packaged birdseed, either. So if you want a beautiful robin or two to make their nests close to your home where you can easily observe us at leisure, the last thing you should be considering is a busy bird table with all those comings and goings.

By the way, this is not just my selfish opinion. There's been a proper scientific study, they reckon, revealing that birds' nests are far more likely to be raided by predators when close to feeding stations or bird tables. The nearer they are, moreover, the more likely this tendency becomes. It stands to reason if you think about it because if there are excessive numbers of squabbling jays and thieving magpies being attracted to your garden, marauding around the bird table and eating everything in sight, it's far more likely they will spot the nests of other smaller birds like ours. Our protein-rich eggs are just an extension of the feeding station for them, and a nice freshly laid robin's egg or two goes down very well for afters, thank you. And that's the problem.

It's up to you, of course. You can have fancy feeding stations if you want, with multitudes of birds and squirrels scrambling for nuts and seeds and mealworms – along with all the rats and mice picking up the crumbs at the end of the day. But if you want some classy visitors to your garden, and that naturally includes happy robins, I suggest establishing a more *bespoke* feeding experience. This is not difficult to achieve with a little imagination – by creating a subtle and discreet space where you can leave just a modest quantity of food each time, and featuring those items robins like best – especially in times of need (in winter, that is, not summer).

In this context, we much prefer to forage discreetly at ground level rather than leaping about on bird tables. A nice flowerpot or logpile where you can scatter food around on the soil beneath the foliage is ideal. We will soon get to know it's there, don't worry, and you can watch us and enjoy our company just the same from your windows or patio. We won't be advertising your efforts to other birds in a hurry, you can be sure of that – and we'll eat up all the crumbs afterwards too.

A bespoke feeding station for robins

Here, above, is a fine example – a nice round potful of tall plants with a good piece of exposed soil to the fore where food can be placed.

Some well-intentioned errors

Robins, as you've probably gathered by this stage, are refined, sophisticated birds with a delicate palette. We're nothing like those huge scavengers, those crows or jackdaws for example that will eat anything. So, regarding the kinds of things you might be considering putting out for us, here if you don't mind are one or two cautionary tales that should be heeded.

Nuts are OK for birds, though unless they are chopped fine robins aren't all that keen on them. But even then it's a terrible error to put out salted ones. Peanuts with salt, for instance, will leave birds dehydrated and feeling thirsty. And there might not be any water around at the time to remedy matters. Too much salt in the diet is not good for humans, so think what it can do to a tiny robin. It could be a matter of life or death.

Leftovers from the kitchen are a good option, you might assume. And, indeed, mostly they are. However, do make sure any bread you give us is reasonably fresh and dry. Damp or soggy old food can be a breeding ground for harmful bacteria and can become mouldy very quickly. Mould on bread can prove fatal to a robin. Similarly, do please make sure any of those scraps do not contain excessive amounts of oil. If the food has been fried it's probably not a great idea giving it to a robin. The oil, even a modest amount, could upset our bowels. If we get the runs and become seriously dehydrated as a result, it could also prove fatal.

Finally, do please check to make sure the crumbs of unwanted cake or mince pies you have left over at Christmas don't contain alcohol. Many festive foods do. Just a trace of alcohol can prove harmful to a small garden bird. Check the labels please – and also look out for any excessive presence of chemical additives, colours or flavourings. These can upset us too, just like they can with humans – their effect being magnified many times over on a small sensitive creature like a robin. Which brings me nicely to a very interesting topic indeed: the senses.

Senses – sight

Robins have all the senses you do: sight, hearing, smell, taste and touch, only some of these are a little sharper and better developed than yours. Sight is a pretty obvious one. One of the reasons a handsome robin like me is so appealing is that I have such very large eyes compared to most other birds. And because those eyes are placed somewhat to the sides of my head, they also provide me with excellent peripheral vision. I can more or less see behind me without needing to turn at all, something that comes in handy for keeping a watch out for any mischievous cats that might be creeping up on me. So it wouldn't be far off the mark to describe us robins as having eyes in the back of our heads.

The only limitation, in common with most creatures, is our ability to look upwards, hence that rather appealing trait that you all like so much when robins tilt their heads to observe the sky. Very cute, yes – but also highly practical because we're usually checking for nasty predators on the wing, like hawks or kestrels.

I suppose in appearance all robins might seem the same to you, but I can recognise other robins easily and distinguish their features even at a distance. Meanwhile, those unusually large eyes also allow me to see clearly in poor light. This is advantageous since it means I can stay up just that little bit later than most other birds, feeding longer, and then get busy the next morning before the others are up and about. I can perceive colour very well, by the way, and it plays a big part in my life – being especially aroused by red, as you know.

Hearing

But what about hearing? Well, being so famously tuneful and full of song, hearing is also obviously a very important sense for robins, and we do have ears just like you do. They are located just to the rear of our faces, but they don't have floppy lobes that stick out like yours, and they are always covered in feathers – particularly tiny and fine feathers, so you don't see them at all.

Robin ears, however, are remarkably sensitive and efficient organs. To hear the soft-pounding paws from a cat about to pounce can be very useful, while our audible senses are also vital to the whole process of song, including that of courtship and the demarcation of our territory. We rely on them to detect the presence even at considerable distances of rival robins.

Naturally, in this context, we are particularly adept at picking up high frequencies – all those tweets and sibilances: the essence of birdsong, much of which is far above the range of human hearing. Thus, what might sound like a pleasant jumble of high-pitched notes to human ears is, to a robin, a well-structured symphony of sound, full of finely crafted trills and cadenzas.

Smell

We don't have a great sense of smell. 'Just as well,' Mrs Robin said to me the other day (I wonder what she meant by that?) At any rate, the olfactory system is certainly not our forte, and it's no better or no worse than that of many other creatures.

Location of the nostrils
just at the base of the
beak

Location of the ears,
covered by fine feathers

The location of robin ears and nostrils

As you can see from the illustration, our nostrils are located at the base of our beaks, just where the beak emerges from the facial feathers. You might sometimes see them referred to as 'nares' by scholars, coming from the Latin word for nostrils. These are about the closest to anything resembling a robin nose. But I think they are rather attractive actually.

Taste

Similarly modest in performance is our sense of taste, which although always active is not particularly well-developed. The cynical among you might well conclude that this is an advantage considering the kinds of things we often have to eat when food is scarce. Shrivelled and rotting old berries aren't renowned for their wholesome fragrances it's true. And as I mentioned before, certain creatures, including most definitely butterflies or certain caterpillars, can taste bad to me, which is a helpful warning sign that they might upset my tummy if I were to swallow them.

Sixth Sense

What is really special about us robins though, and which you might find quite exciting and certainly admirable, is a kind of sixth sense that comes to the fore at times of migration, the subtle art that birds possess of travelling over long distances. You see, some robins migrate overseas for a few months in the winter. They journey to warmer climes, and when they return from hundreds of miles away they often do so to the exact same location of their former territory. That's clever, and it relies in part on that amazing sixth sense – of which I shall have much more to tell you in the next chapter concerning autumn, because the subject of migration is definitely on the agenda then (at least for some of us).

Finally, just a word about the tactile senses. Like most wild creatures we are generally very sensitive to touch, especially our beaks and tongues, which are able to detect all sorts of different textures and subtle movements that help us in catching prey and, at moments, holding stuff delicately in our bills while we pick up additional items. That's a skill that definitely comes in handy when conveying beakfuls of food to the nest and feeding our young.

All that sensitivity can be a mixed blessing, however, because it can also keep our attention returning again and again to some of the more irritating distractions that summer brings to a robin – namely a number of persistent itches that we will succumb to at various times. Yes, I'm afraid we must now turn to a somewhat delicate subject – one that with brutal honesty can only be described as parasitic infestations. *Ugh!*

Nasty bugs and parasites

Because robins are clever enough not to use the same nesting material twice in a season like some foolish birds, we tend not to be affected too badly by fleas. And our solitary lifestyle and tendency not to mix too much with other birds, means we rarely succumb to infectious diseases. But there are other problems to contend with. A serious bane on robins and a torment we have to endure regularly during the warm weather is the presence of numerous annoying little critters that lodge themselves under our feathers or sometimes even into the shafts of the feathers themselves. These are lice and they specialise in nibbling away at old discarded feather material, or maybe even laying their eggs within the shafts of our precious feathers as part of their breeding cycle.

You hardly notice them at first, and for a healthy bird like me, the problem rarely gets out of hand; but as the warm weather comes on apace, and especially if a bird is elderly or sick, the parasites can proliferate and become a real nuisance. They are so tiny we can't always dislodge them with our beaks, or flush them out with water when we bathe. And they can make us itch like mad!

There are also other nasty things called 'tics' – horrid little parasites that hook themselves onto our skin and subsequently gorge themselves on robin blood, swelling up in the process from something almost invisible at first to the size of a small pea. They drop off eventually once they've had their fill. But can you imagine how horrible that feels?

Fungal Infections and worms

Fungal infections can also add to the discomfort that robins – and many other birds – experience during the summer months. For instance, you might sometimes see a robin with a curious bald patch above or around its eyes. This usually comes as a result of an itchy fungal growth. Scratching it again and again with our talons causes the baldness. And if all that wasn't bad enough, we can even fall victim to internal worm infestations.

By worms I don't mean the nice tasty ones sticking out of the lawn that robins eat, but the ever-so-tiny ones which we ingest somehow with our food or pick up from the ground itself. Again, these can be so small that even a sharp-eyed robin like me cannot see them, and they can easily be ingested before taking up residence in the gut. They can harm us there, drawing on our energies and sapping our strength. They can even enter the blood stream and damage our internal organs, our lungs and our livers.

Really, what a nuisance it all is! I don't think these are very noble creatures, do you? Parasites – I don't know how they can live with themselves sometimes, with so much suffering on their consciences. Anyway, the upshot of all this is to let you know that there are some pretty weird and disagreeable little creatures out here we're obliged to share our lives with, and they have some pretty eccentric ways about them.

Mind you, robins can be eccentric at times as well and we can have some unusual methods of going about keeping ourselves well – especially when retaliating against those blood-sucking parasites. I shall let you into a rather intriguing little secret next about one of the ways we go about it.

Robins' anting antics

So, here's a confession for you. You might conclude that what I'm about to tell you is a bit odd, but I like nothing more when I have a little leisure time than finding myself a nice active colony of ants, perhaps the occupants of a nice busy anthill somewhere in the garden, and then I'll play about among them. Yes, seriously!

It's not because I necessarily want to eat the ants. Rather, the unique procedure of 'anting' as it is called is something that several bird species incorporate occasionally into their routine of personal grooming. And it really is a great help, because the ants, when disturbed or when they feel threatened like this, emit a really useful chemical called formic acid, which birds are grateful for because it cleanses our feathers and kills many of the horrible bugs and parasites that might have taken up residence there. It's like soap and disinfectant for robins.

Sometimes, wanting to be a little more forensic about the process, I will pick up an ant and trail his body through my wing feathers, and it will spray a little bit of formic acid onto them just where I need it most. It feels nice too, in a funny sort of way and the whole thing can become quite addictive. The ant isn't too pleased about it of course, but never mind. The main thing is that the formic acid it releases is anathema to many of those lice and ticks that I mentioned a moment ago – and any number of other unpleasant parasites that birds in the wild can succumb to.

I once even bellyfloppped onto an anthill, with a whole crowd of teeming ants and let them crawl all over me. A bit extreme, I know, but it's easy to shake them off when necessary and it certainly did the trick. No more itches after that – at least not for a while.

I say 'not for a while' because there are other far more significant changes that occur with our feathers at this time of the year, changes that can prove particularly distressing – especially for a young bird when it happens for the first time – and against which all the ants in the world are of no use whatsoever. What am I referring to? The dreaded Moult, that's what – and it always takes place towards the end of summer whether we like it or not.

Let me tell you all about this next.

The Moult Cometh

Have you ever wondered why you don't see robins so often in summer as compared to the rest of the year? Sometimes it seems as if we have simply vanished from the face of the earth. I can understand why you might think that, since we do tend to keep a low profile. But we really are here all the while, just the same as ever.

You will as a matter of course notice us far less amid the colourful summer garden, anyway – conspicuously less than during, say, the drab old days of winter when our red breast stands out amid the gloom. But the onset of the moulting season now at the height of summer is also a very persuasive reason for us to keep out of sight.

The process of losing of our old feathers to be replaced like-for-like with new ones, occurs annually when our existing ones simply drop out. Even our precious tail and wing feathers that are so essential for proper balance and flight, they fall out too. And that's no laughing matter. It's a wretched period, extremely embarrassing, wholly debilitating and a scourge on our overall happiness and well being that can last anything up to six weeks or longer – and you really just want to hide away until it's all over.

As you might recall from the earlier chapter on winter, birds like us will have several different types of feathers: the soft downy ones under the chest and tummy that help keep us warm; and the powerful flight feathers of our wings, responsible for lifting and propulsion, and which present themselves in overlapping layers when the wings are folded by our sides. Among these are the long feathers that are termed 'primaries' attached to our hands; the so-called 'secondaries' attached to our forearms, and the 'tertials' nearer to our robin shoulders.

And as you can see from the illustration, there are, in addition to the long flight feathers of the arms and hands, a whole group of shorter ones called 'coverts', which cover the leading edge of the wing and help provide a typical aerodynamic shape.

Taken all together they make for a beautiful array when extended in flight.

Feathers of the wing
showing the top of right-hand wing

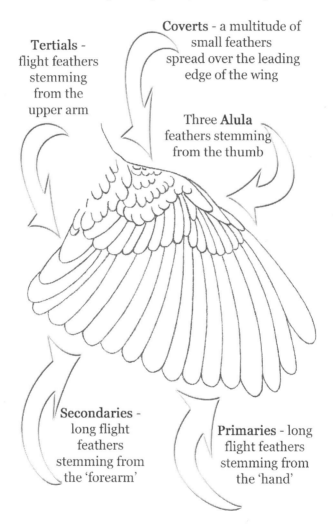

Tertials -
flight feathers
stemming
from the
upper arm

Coverts - a multitude of
small feathers
spread over the leading
edge of the wing

Three **Alula**
feathers stemming
from the thumb

Secondaries -
long flight
feathers
stemming from
the 'forearm'

Primaries - long
flight feathers
stemming from
the 'hand'

A wing and its feathers

Most obvious, also, when you look at a fine specimen of a robin like me is my elegant tail feathers, presenting as a fan-shaped array when open and originating from what seems almost like an extension of the spine. These are essential for balance, both in flight and on the ground and also for steering while in flight. Finally, in this by no means exhaustive list, there are special contour feathers on my back and numerous, almost hair-like ones on the face and around the eyes.

Many different structures – but what they all have in common is their growth cycle, that they stem from a multitude of tiny outcrops on the skin, similar in a way to the follicles at the roots of human or animal hair. Birds don't have hair, of course, and once a feather has grown to its full size it does not keep growing like hair does. There's no need for a trim at the barbers or hairdressers to keep a robin looking smart during the course of the year. We're just expected to wait until our old feathers fall out and become renewed during these long forty or fifty embarrassing days towards the end of summer.

Fortunately they don't all go at once. Moulting is a gradual process of replacement, proceeding in an orderly though staggered fashion. That's why it takes so long. So if I start to lose feathers during, say, the early days of July, it might not be until the start of September that I'll be returning to anything approaching my normal resplendent appearance.

Some of the inner primary feathers of the wings are the first to go. Then, as these begin to be replaced with new ones, some of the outer ones will drop away – again being replaced in turn with new. The feathers of the secondaries meanwhile are replaced in the reverse order, from the outside inwards. All this ensures that we are never entirely without feathers of some kind, and so are not seriously incapacitated at any stage regarding flight – a gradual and well-ordered procedure causing the least possible disruption.

So, now you know: that's where robins disappear to in the summer. That's why we're compelled to go against our natural inclinations and cease showing off for a while. And it always occurs at around the same time of every year, regular as clockwork. And, of course, the results are really rather splendid once it's all over.

Robins falling silent

As you can well appreciate by now, the moulting season is a pretty dismal period for a proud robin. What with having a horrible ragbag of feathers hanging about and half a tail to be getting on with; what with all the mating and nesting excitement behind us, and the young being off hand and soon to experience a partial moult of their own as they grow towards adulthood, the very end of summer can be quite a dull period for robins. There are lots of other bird species, moreover, who are obliged to endure the same inconvenience, albeit at slightly different times of the year.

Invisibility as well as silence

And so it is now when you might also notice a strange silence descending on the garden or countryside, as we robins all at once decide to pack up singing. All that noisy, combative vocalising that you enjoyed while we were establishing our territory in winter and finding a mate in spring, and even those few days of singing to our young fledglings so they learn a few vocal tricks to serve them in adulthood, it all fades away now. Reluctantly, brave robins must, at least for a while, become the strong silent types and as a consequence perhaps just a little melancholic as well.

Really - it seems so unfair. Just look at that skylark out there, singing away as he climbs higher and higher into the sky. Not a care in the world. And just look at all those magnificent feathers! How come he still has all of his?

Robin pondering a skylark

Fledglings to juvenile, a transformation

As we have seen, our young robins will have their flight feathers pretty well developed by the time they are about 20 days old – that is after being out of the nest for a little under a week. They no longer need to hop about to escape danger by then but can easily leave the ground and shoot up into trees. But their flight is still far from accomplished, and they still don't look like proper adult robins just yet. When does that eminent red breast start to appear, you might well ask? Well, it's not too far off.

In late summer, if they have managed to survive, our juvenile robins as they should now be called will experience a moult too – a change of feathers round about the same time as the adult birds have their more extensive change. In the case of the juveniles, it's not a full moult because their spanking-new flight feathers will not require replacement until next year. But what does occur now is a no-less-important partial moult during which they finally gain their adult body plumage, including that brilliant red breast. They are becoming proper robins now. They can go their own way. And we, the parents, can certainly take it easy and stop feeding the little rascals.

In former times, people used to get the idea that the adult birds would drive out the younger ones, or that the youngsters would even turn against the oldens and attack them. None of these wild assertions is true. Robins from the same family tolerate one another quite well. There is an essential learning curve for the juvenile robins to go through in any case, and they need their parents for this. An easy coexistence reigns – at least until the winter months when the new round of territorial claims start to take place in earnest.

So, even though life can be pretty traumatic and unsettling at moments during these late-summer days, it's not all bad. Because there's always one activity guaranteed to perk us up and stop us feeling sorry for ourselves, and that's a good bit of pampering from a long cool session in the birdbath.

The joys of bathing

I have, I believe, explained already in the chapter on winter about how important it is for us robins to have access to fresh drinking water during the cold winter months, and how very much we appreciate it if you maintain a spare bowl outside or a birdbath with fresh, clean water in it for us to bathe. But birdbaths also really come into their own right now in the lazy closing days of summer. I just love having a soak at this time of the year. Some days you can hardly keep me out of the birdbath it's so much fun splashing around in the water.

As well as being useful in aiding the vital process of preening, bathing really is one of life's great pleasures. Sometimes, when it's very late and all the other birds have gone to sleep, I even pop in and have a dip in the moonlight – or at other times go in together with Mrs Robin, and we take it in turns to have a good splash around. Cor – wonderful! I can get quite passionate about it, actually. Those warm, tranquil evenings have a strange kind of serenity to them don't they? And life doesn't get much better than this. Makes me come over all poetic sometimes.

> *'No one knows,*
> *And no one sees.*
> *At dusk we come*
> *To bathe our little robin knees.'*

All right: I know. Not exactly *Ode to a Nightingale*, but I don't think it's too bad for a robin.

~ ~ ~

It is the year's maturity now, and everything is settled and gloriously calm – our robin voices replaced with murmurous bees and the languid sounds of crickets in long grass. On the edges of fields cattle recline in shade and flick at flies with their restless tails. Watching them can be quite mesmerising for a robin, and there's not much else for me to do anyway – as if time is standing still. It's a spell that's only ever broken by something sudden like a thunderstorm. Those are amazing when they come along – terrifying – with those great clouds that climb and rumble up from nowhere so quickly and with winds and driving rain that startles us and makes us fly to cover. Storms with hailstones thrown in are the worst for birds like us. Can you imagine how big those seem to a tiny robin? And how very heavy too, if one hits us on the head?

Yes: the end of summer. How lovely it has been (most of the time, anyway). You sometimes think it's never going to end. But of course it does. All things must. And so it's the shortening days of autumn I shall tell you of next. And although you might think that's a gloomy prospect, it can be quite an agreeable season for robins, at least at the start. That's because in autumn there's always so much sweet fruit around to eat. And that's important because we need to fatten up. Yes, really we do!

Any excuse.

Robin in Autumn

AUTUMN

The onset of autumn is upon us, and it seems to have arrived particularly early this year. The weather is getting gloomy; the nights are drawing in and some of the youngsters are already starting to complain. 'You'll have to get used to it,' I tell them. 'It happens every year.'

They'll learn.

Yes, autumn. Some consider it a sad time. They become dispirited now that the long, verdant days are over. But I rather like it. The weather is not all that chilly yet, and the youngsters are grown up and not at all demanding any longer. So, yes, it really can be quite an acceptable time of year – strangely liberating. And there's also something delightfully *'gothic'* about autumn, too, don't you think? Yes, I reckon I'm a bit of a goth-robin at heart. Maybe I should start cultivating a new image and become a bit more moody and mysterious? I wonder what Mrs Robin will make of *that?*

What robins of all persuasions certainly do like at this time of the year, though, is that there's often a good strong breeze to be had. Full of vigour and mischief, it whistles and dances and reaches into every proud corner of the garden, stirring up all the debris along the paths and borders and revealing lots of little wrigglies for me to sample – ones that I might not normally have been able to find. Always something new to discover in autumn. It's just so exciting.

And look: spiders, *spiders* everywhere! Some small and manageable; others as big as saucers, or so it seems if you are just a tiny robin. But I don't object to those either. They don't mean us any harm. And all those dainty mini-spiders definitely came in handy a couple of months ago as I recall for feeding our youngsters when they were unable to swallow very much at first. And though it can be a real nuisance when the cobwebs get tangled round your beak, I am still more than a little partial to them even now.

What is a real delight at this time of the year however is the prospect of so many varieties of berries and fruits: delicious sweet food for robins that literally grows on trees (and doesn't run away when you try to eat it). There are lots of these colourful delights in the gardens now, gardens that are also ablaze with golden chrysanthemums, red fuchsias and purple Michaelmas daisies. It's all bright and brassy everywhere: just as robins like it.

Yes, fruits and berries are the real treats of autumn and I shall tell you later in this chapter just how you can help us robins in this respect by growing more of the kinds of trees and shrubs whose fruits we relish the most.

The end of a fine romance

The early days of autumn can be poignant ones because they mark the time when robins previously paired for mating and nesting begin to lose their attraction to one another and start to go their separate ways. In fact it all happens rather suddenly. Both males and females now set themselves the target once more of establishing their own individual territories. The sense of having a shared purpose ebbs away; much of the romance vanishes and things can start to get ... a bit *edgy*. It's sad really, because I used to be so fond of my Mrs Robin, and we have been through such a lot together all year long, but now ... well, she gets all grumpy when I'm close by, and even tells me off sometimes for singing too loudly. Imagine that!

The youngsters meanwhile can certainly make their own way in the world by this time. Or let me put that another way – they'd better, *or else!* As parents, we can both get a bit stroppy if the juveniles keep bothering us for food when they are self-sufficient and can perfectly well shake their feathers up and fend for themselves. And although we do recognise them still as family and we would never harm them, they will eventually become stronger and more independent, until one day they might even come to regard us, their own parents, as interlopers. How's that for gratitude!

That probably won't be for a while yet though. Next year, maybe. Then it'll be every robin for themselves.

Robin thoughts

So, seeing us like this with so much leisure time at our disposal, I suppose you might be wondering what robins think about during these increasingly frequent moments of solitude and idleness. Well, I would like to remind you at this point that robins are actually quite intelligent birds. Oh yes. And we really do a lot of thinking about things: about worms and where to find them, for example, or the whereabouts of any number of other dainty morsels to pop into our beaks. We are very alert creatures too, and I must say I do rather object to the disparaging term 'bird brain' that so many people bandy about. This is just insulting in my opinion and highly inaccurate in any case.

Let me tell you something. It's a well known fact that in autumn, if I choose, I can migrate – that is to fly off hundreds of miles to another part of the world, and then return a few months later to the exact same spot from which I started. How's that for mental dexterity?

Or, on the other hand, if I decide to stay at home, and when those strong autumn winds come along, as they surely will very soon, I could for instance be out here at night having to sleep in a force seven gale backing from a south-easterly all the way round the west in the course of a few hours, with driving rain, hailstones and the occasional rumble of thunder thrown in for good measure, and yet my brain has told me how to choose just the right place to shelter, so I can safely cling to my chosen branch all night without once toppling. Then I'm up the next morning at sunrise, probably long before you are, having my breakfast. How many people you know who go about dropping the term 'bird brain' could manage *that*, I wonder? Huh! Many a human should envy such a brain in my opinion.

And another thing: we can become quite cultured in our ways too – especially when living near to people ... well, *some* people anyway (unfortunately we can't always choose). And robins, like most birds, are not averse to good music either. I often listen to it through people's windows, especially if it's relevant and has a food connotation. My favourites are the beetles (have I spelt that right?) and I do enjoy a bit of the highbrow stuff too. Verdi for instance – those famous operas of his. What's that one he did? *Wriggeletto?* That's a good one.

Migration – for a few of us, anyway

With the onset of the shortening days of autumn, things get shaken up among your typical robin population – especially with regard to how we set out our boundaries between individual territories. At first, these seem not quite as strict as they once were during the breeding season, and a lot of us robins continue to wander and explore as we did in the late days of summer, perhaps even considering a change of scene and establishing a fresh territory elsewhere, especially if an attractive vacancy has occurred nearby. Not only that, but as the weather deteriorates some robins become so restless that they even decide to go away completely. It might just be a mile or two from their present territory or it could be a major undertaking – that migration I mentioned, and the flying off all the way to somewhere like France or Spain.

You see, robins are just like people. Some of us just can't face the prospect of struggling through a long cold winter at home. So round about, say, the middle of autumn they opt for a holiday overseas. Not everyone goes, of course. Perhaps only as little as one in thirty of us, but right now it's the big talking point around here amongst us robins: who's thinking of going, who's staying. Gossip abounds.

It's mainly the female robins who elect to go, by the way, and so – again - the shift can bring about some notable changes in the dynamics of the local robin population, with territorial boundaries becoming even more flexible. Not only do we miss familiar robin faces that we have come to know so well, but to add to the mix of confusion, foreign robins from areas like Scandinavia or the Netherlands will fly over to Britain to take their places here. The weather must be pretty cold there for them to do that, but I suppose all creatures like a change of scene anyway.

Navigation

The ability to navigate over distance as many bird species do is a great asset and is one of those unique faculties whose nature is yet to be fully unlocked by people who study our ways. For us, though, we hardly give it a second thought. We just spread our wings and go. In the case of robin migration this is often commenced at night. In so doing we make use of prominent landmarks and coastlines or by looking at the sky to find our direction. By day, it's the position of the sun, while after dark we use the moon and stars – all more or less without thinking about it.

Also, experts have discovered that to aid us even further we have a kind of built-in compass, a tiny amount of a substance called magnetite located in our skulls that gives us a special sensitivity to the earth's magnetic field. And all these cues in combination make up what you might properly call that 'sixth sense' that I mentioned in chapter three. It's this that allows us to cover enormous distances to far-away places and, even more remarkably a few months later, to steer ourselves right back again to the very same spot from where we started without getting lost.

When to go?

For robins the decision of when to leave is a personal matter. We don't gather in flocks like starlings or swallows, making a great song and dance of it before going off all at once, but instead each robin will quietly weigh up the conditions and decide for his or herself when the moment is right to depart, if at all.

Typical Winter Robin Migration
to and from the UK

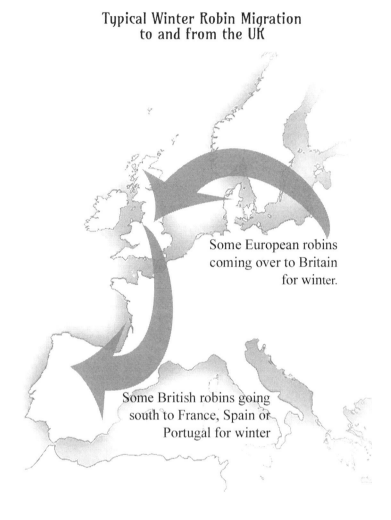

Some European robins
coming over to Britain
for winter.

Some British robins going
south to France, Spain or
Portugal for winter

Approximate pattern of annual robin migration

This is an important call. At the best of times it can be a dangerous journey, and for all our special skills and talents, even if we reach our destination in one piece, we really can't do much about ignorant people who catch robins in nets when we land or, worse, shoot us for 'sport' as we fly overhead. Yes, that really does happen on the continent.

Sadly, therefore, not every robin will return from its romantic sojourn overseas. But there you are! Despite all the hazards and all the terrible unpredictability of winds and storms, hunters and predators, there's no way you can persuade some robins against it, not once they've made up their minds. My Mrs Robin is a bit like that, and it looks as though this year she will be off gallivanting again. She says Portugal looks very tempting this time around. *Portugal!*

If you ask me, I reckon the moult has a lot to do with it. You see, robins are proud birds, and having endured that dreadful period looking really grim at the end of summer, some robins feel they need a bit of a treat and a change of scene.

'Fine feathers make fine birds,' says Mrs Robin. And as soon as the moult is over and she has her new plumage, all glossy and beautiful, she'll be off.

Well ... all right for some, I suppose, but to be frank most of us males aren't bothered about travelling too far from home. And certainly not going off abroad like that. All that foreign food. I mean, you can't even get a decent worm over in some of those places, the ground is so dry. No ... we prefer to stay right here where we feel more comfortable, and to concentrate on recuperating after all that hard graft and family business during the summer.

There are plenty of changes taking place in the

countryside now anyway, and that's always interesting to observe. Much of the woodland and garden foliage starts to dry up and fall away, and you really can begin to see the shapes of all those giant trees again – trees that once seemed so vast and that only just a few weeks ago would have covered us with shade. A stubborn old oak or two might retain its leaves a little longer than the rest, all brown and crinkly, but their branches are almost bare by the end of October and a robin can see where he's going, taking in the wider picture. I can pop up onto the highest of my perches now and sing away knowing that the whole world can *see* as well as hear me. That's living.

Singing strikes up again

Yes, singing again. As stated earlier, unlike many birds, robins sing almost all year round, the only exception being, as we have seen, during the moulting period of late summer. But with the passing of the equinox and the shortening days we are beginning to find our voices once more and also considering re-establishing some of our former boundaries.

In truth, I suppose none of us are overly fussed about that sort of thing just yet, and next year's nesting season certainly seems a long way off. But it is a prospect that will become more and more significant as the weeks go by.

Funny thing, birdsong. People have always been fascinated by it. But still, even now, after listening to us and observing us all these years in the wild, after following us around, watching us through binoculars, putting rings on our feet and recording our songs, *still* you haven't got a clue what we're actually singing about, have you? Go on, admit it! You just don't know.

Consequently, some experts can be dismissive of the whole thing. They reckon all this singing lark is probably not only silly but completely unnecessary at this time of the year. After all, they say, we don't need to sing to keep other robins away from our food supplies, because there's ample food everywhere right now. And we don't need to sing to get a mate either, because all that romancing business is many months into the future with next year's breeding cycle. Yet for all that, still we like to sing. So why?

The answer in a broad sense is that we simply enjoy it. It is our *forte*. We established this principle earlier, as I recall, in chapter one. And the occasional warning tweet to other robins in the vicinity doesn't go amiss at any time, *just in case*. But there is more. Let's look at the subject a bit more closely.

Two types of song

You don't have to be an expert to notice there are two distinct types of robin song. Firstly, there's the really powerful in-your-face defending-my-domain kind of song that I broadcast to all comers during winter and spring. Strong and insistent and hard to ignore, especially if you're another robin. And then, right now as autumn gets under way, there's the much quieter, lyrical singing that you'll hear. It's much more gentle and can go on for ages – having been described, I believe, as a kind of soft, melodious warble.

I do a lot of that, the soft melodious warbling version around about now – even though, as I say, it doesn't have much to do with territorial claims. Much of it is purely whimsical.

Yes, *whimsical*. And there's nothing wrong with that. That's what robins do, especially if there's another robin nearby to hear us, which there almost always is, of course. How can I explain it in human terms? It's a bit like with sport, when two rival fans discuss things in a pub after the game. It can go on for hours, nattering away like this without anyone really saying anything very much at all. And that's just what robins are like in autumn. I'll be singing to that other chap over there in the neighbouring tree about nothing much and he sings back to me about nothing much as well. We aren't too bothered about excessive displays of aggression any longer. There's no need at the moment. But we do both enjoy a chat.

'Turned out nice again, hasn't it,' I sing.

'Yes turned out very nice again today,' he sings back.

'Don't forget to keep off my patch,' I remind him, though rather half-heartedly.

And he says, 'All right, and you keep off my patch too. Don't worry about your Mrs Robin if she goes. She'll be back. *Keep your pecker up!*'

All right, I do appreciate this might all sound a bit shallow, twittering on like that, but to be brutally honest

I've listened to a good amount of human conversation over the years from my perch up in the tree and it really isn't all that much better.

Just occasionally though the exchanges will take on a more educational quality. That new robin over there, for instance, who's very young. He says he's feeling anxious lately and a bit depressed. He's heard that he has to find a lady robin next year and make babies but he's never done anything like that before.

'How do I do it?' he asks.

'Just use your instinct!' I tell him (*funny robin*).

Mysterious robins?

Actually, while we're on the subject of communication, how do you know that all this singing isn't just a bit more sophisticated than mere idle chit chat? How can you be sure, for instance, that robins aren't really quite deep and mysterious creatures that need to communicate their feelings to other robins by making use of a complex language all of our own, embedded in our singing? Why, some of us might even sound remarkably eloquent and poetic to the ears of another robin. Take me, for example. In my spare time I might be highly proficient in the avian equivalent of a Shakespearean sonnet – yes, that's right: composing at this very moment some beautiful rhyming verse to my Mrs Robin before she goes away. *'Shall I compare thee to a wriggly worm?'* and things like that. Just so she'll know what she's missing.

Roosting

I explained to you earlier in the chapter on winter about how we manage to survive at night even in the coldest conditions, but have you ever wondered exactly what sort of places robins go for sleeping or 'roosting' as we should call it? Well, as with most birds it varies a lot according to the weather and the wind direction. We like a sheltered position and if it's raining a reasonably dry one too. A nice thick bush or well-covered tree is preferable – anywhere where we can get a grip on a branch with those strong talons of ours and settle down for the night out of harm's way.

There are usually lots of spots to choose from and I must say I've become very partial of late to a particularly fragrant rosemary bush. It rarely gets investigated by the foxes and badgers, and it doesn't half make your feathers smell nice in the morning! The other robins are very impressed ... *I think.*

One thing you might be surprised to learn is that even though robins wake early and like to start their day before most other birds – sometimes even before sunrise – we don't always sleep right through from dusk to dawn. Sometimes we sing even in the dark. Now that is just a bit unusual, isn't it? Let me tell you all about this next.

Nocturnal Songsters

Not everyone has heard us, but some robins do sing at night. Yes, it really does happen – especially if there's a big full moon or we find ourselves close to artificial light. Some urban robins sing by the light of street lamps or floodlights and can become addicted to the stimulus of late nights – while some particularly accomplished songsters among us can even have their efforts mistaken for those of a nightingale. That really is a compliment because as anyone who has ever been fortunate enough to hear a nightingale will testify, theirs is the most beautiful song of all.

A robin is often described by naturalists as having big beady eyes. That's a bit of a nerve, isn't it? But it is certainly true that we have quite large and prominent eyes compared to other birds, which inclines us to be very handsome and appealing as a consequence. Also, as I explained earlier, it's thanks to this feature that we can see pretty well late into the evening too.

It's then when you'll notice us in the twilight scurrying about for that final morsel of food, long after all the other birds have gone to roost. It also means that we can begin hunting early in the morning before it's fully light and while most other birds are still slumbering. Like the proverb says: it's the early bird that catches the worm. And consequently it is the garden robin whose voice is often the prelude to those wonderful dawn choruses that you hear in spring and summer – the wake-up call to all those other dozy birds.

It would certainly be fair to say, therefore, that robins (and birds generally) are highly sensitive and deeply rooted in the cycles of nature. We have to be. We must be alert to the timing of sunrises and sunsets; to the changing lengths of the daylight hours; to the passage of the days and the seasons and to the patterns of weather and the movements of the sun, the moon and the stars – all things that we need not just for waking early but for getting through our day safely too. And, of course, our astronomical senses really do come to the fore when navigating long distances in the dark.

Robins were observers of the heavens and the night sky long before humans.

'At night I wake
With stars in the sky,
And sing to Endymion,
As the Moon sails by.'

Sociability

Although English robins are not all that keen when other robins intrude on their patch – especially during the mating season (show me another red-breasted robin in spring and I find myself getting rather cross, as you know), we are actually very tolerant of other bird species and will happily share our ground with them most times of the year. For instance, if perchance a little wren were to hop across the boundary into my space I probably wouldn't mind in the least, even in spring. We might even form an alliance and watch out for each other while we feed. And blackbirds and thrushes, our cousins, are invariably welcome neighbours.

We also like people, of course. It's a very well-known

fact about the British robin in particular: our friendliness towards humans, and a trait distinct from our European counterparts whose behaviour is more than a little at variance to ours. Over there, on the continent, where robins are sometimes hunted and eaten by people, they have become naturally reticent and shy. Whereas here in the UK, robins are well respected and protected by law. Yes, from the 19th century to the present day there have been Acts of Parliament passed to protect us birds, and sometimes specifically to protect robins and our eggs. Go against those and you'll soon be up before the beak. But even without laws and regulations, most folks here in the UK are generally kind to robins. They always have been (and they don't eat us, either).

Perhaps that is why your resident robin is normally so tame and is one of the few species of birds who can actually be coaxed into feeding from your hand: if you're patient enough. Perhaps, too, it's because English robins are just naturally courageous. Fearless is perhaps a better term. Fearless without being reckless, that's us: the very spirit of Old Albion. And those robins who do migrate for a few months take our pleasant ways with them too. So, in the unlikely event that anyone in France or Spain has a handful of tasty mealworms or raisins to offer us when we arrive ... well, quite frankly we're anybody's!

By the same token, you can always spot one of those continental robins if they chance to migrate from, say, Scandinavia or Germany to the UK during the winter, because they are just the reverse to us in temperament.

That's why, if you ever notice that your local garden robin has suddenly started to behave oddly and not at all like itself, it's probably because it isn't your local robin anyway but an impostor from afar who just happens to look very similar. You'll find this sad little creature, if you can find it at all, hiding in the most remote corners of your garden or skulking around in the hedgerows and thickets. They won't come near people hardly at all. Miserable lot! We're not sorry to see the back of them at the end of winter – a time that coincides with the return of our own lovely lady robins, of course, flying back from their holiday adventures in the south – looking all glamorous and ready for the new year. Happy days.

I do miss Mrs Robin now she's gone. And of course robins don't even send postcards or anything like that to let others know how they're getting on. I worry because, as I mentioned earlier, it's certainly not all sunshine and delight for migrating robins, even if they do negotiate the journey safely – and not exactly free of care either once they get there, since they will soon be faced with a tough decision concerning just when they should return. And in this respect it is the weather back here at home that is the big unknown factor.

Think about it for a moment. If your typical migrating female returns too soon in the new year, she might only come back to find jack frost or thick snow on the ground to welcome her. It will be difficult therefore to find food. If on the other hand she leaves it too late, then all the best and most handsome male robins will already be spoken for and paired up. So she has to get the timing just right. A big ask.

Gluttony – yes, but not from choice

Did you know that a bird like me needs to eat at least a quarter of its body weight each day to maintain its weight? Honestly. More in winter – perhaps as much as one third more. That's a lot of grub, believe me. And it's partly because of these demands that autumn proves to be such a rewarding time for robins – not least of all because now, with all the stresses of summer and the rearing of our young being over, we can really settle down at last to just pleasing ourselves and, most importantly of all, *eating*.

I know it might all seem rather greedy and self-indulgent, but eating and storing up a good layer of fat is really more important now than ever for us robins with the imminent prospect of much colder weather on the way. We know that doing so provides us with energy to spare, since we can burn off those excess calories for a few days to keep warm if the weather turns really chilly.

Even for those more-adventurous robins who have decided to fly off overseas, a good store of fat will have been essential in order to cover the distances involved (as you know, it can be hundreds of miles). A strong, healthy robin thus fortified can usually manage this in one go without having to land anywhere at all. There's stamina for you!

Whatever the reason though, autumn is definitely the season for putting on weight, a task I've always found quite easy to achieve, as it happens, and I have to admit the girth has increased a little of late. Mrs Robin, before she went off, had even taken to calling me *Jumbo* –

which I don't think was at all kind do you?

Of course, it's all right for migrating robins to go on like that. They're off to somewhere warm. The rest of us have the prospect of a freezing British winter staring us in the face. And that's no joke. And I'll tell you something else, no robin ever died by tucking away a little extra on the ribs at this time of the year.

Anyway, who wouldn't be just a tad self-indulgent at present with so many delicious and succulent varieties of food to discover? It must have been awful to have been a caged bird in olden times. People really used to do that – to shut us in like that. Terrible.

> 'A Robin Red Breast in a Cage
> Puts all Heaven in a Rage'
>
> *William Blake*

Yes liberty is sweet, appreciated least until it is lost. And how wonderful just to be able to go anywhere I fancy! Some of my favourite autumn snacks I go exploring for right now come in the shape of those nice spindly crane flies. Daddy-long-legs, some people call them. You can spot them easily on a new-mown lawn or around the edges of fields. Funny things: they are so slow and plodding. They flutter up and down or hover above the grass just waiting to be gobbled up. I love leaping around the garden catching them on the wing, which might sound a bit callous, I suppose – but gardeners take note: I'm doing you a big favour here because those crane flies will soon be laying their eggs, and lots of them, which will quickly transform themselves into leatherjacket larvae that will nibble away at the roots of the grass in your lawns. Unchecked, they become a major pest.

In other words you can rely on a robin to do the right thing (strikes an heroic pose).

The Hungry Robin

MENU

AUTUMN SEASONAL FARE

Earthworms
Beetles & Bugs
~~Caterpillars~~
Spiders - *petit*
Centipedes & Millipedes
Maggots, grubs & larvae
Craneflies

VEGETARIAN

Berries and Rose Hips
Plant and weed seeds (various)
Juicy Windfalls (when available)
Forraged Fruit (gardeners not looking)

DESSERT

Specialities fresh from the bird table

Bread and Biscuit Crumbs
Kibbled Sunflower Hearts
Mealworms

Opening times: sunrise to sunset daily.
Garden Lane, Wrigglesbury, Hunts, AR0 8IN

Autumn season's menu at The Hungry Robin

Yes, lots of lovely worms and assorted wrigglies available still. But, as you can see from the menu, it's the berries and fruits that are to be found in such abundance just about everywhere now that are so tempting. Many of them are sweet, and robins if nothing else do have a weakness for sweet things.

Autumn – season of mellow fruitfulness

So, what, exactly do we eat by way of fruit? Well, in the olden days when robins used to live exclusively in woods and forests (once upon a time almost all parts of the country were covered in deciduous trees and forests) our diet was purely natural. We inhabited the glades and borders of woodland, and in autumn this meant, and still does mean, availing ourselves of the fruits of the season growing there in the sunlight or partial shade.

Even before the onset of autumn and those first hints of a change to cooler temperatures, we start to see the first berries, and from then onwards it's a real feast. Fruits such as mulberry, wild cherry or blackberry are always welcome additions to a robin's diet since many of these contain valuable vitamin C, which helps prevent illness. Others such as rowan or holly, and though probably just as nutritious, might not be quite so palatable or easily digestible, and we're more inclined to leave those for more desperate times – especially us robins who live in the wild, away from gardens and human habitation.

Planting for a robin-friendly garden

Not everyone reading this will have a garden, or even want one. But if you do have charge of a little plot of land, then you can go just that one step further and help robins by deliberately planting more of the kinds of shrubs and trees that we like the most.

A wide choice exists these days – what with garden nurseries and online retailers offering all sorts of exotic specimens. But, in fact, it's best just to keep things simple. Our native UK species of plants or trees like elder or hawthorn are always preferable to exotic varieties from overseas since they already stand a good chance of being naturally suited to the wildlife and soil where you live – while those rare and fancy imported plants that might look great in the catalogues are not always compatible with our UK climate.

There's one notable exception to this rule though. At least I think so – and that's the Cordyline or Cabbage Palm. It might appear a bit exotic, but it's perfectly happy near coasts or in southerly parts of the UK. Mature specimens can bring forth great bunches of delicious crisp little seeds in the autumn. We just can't get enough of those. And I should also just mention the native spindle tree – sometimes referred to as 'robins bread'. We love the tiny fruits of those so much and will defend any territory containing a spindle tree most vigorously. Here is a handy guide as to what robins like best.

Robin's berry-nice star ratings

 Warning: With few exceptions the items in this list are NOT recommended for human consumption. Never eat any wild berry or fruit unless you are absolutely certain of its identity.

Barberries - Spikey plant with abundant berries ★★ 🍃

Blackberry - Early fruiting, but robins love them ★★★★ UK

Blackthorn - Small, purple fruits called 'sloes' ★★ UK

Bullace - The wild plumb or damson ★★★ UK

Dog Rose – Produces nutritious 'hips' in autumn ★★★ UK

Dogwood - Clusters of white berries on red stems ★★ UK

Elder - Attractive white-flowering shrub ★★★★ UK

Firethorn or pyracantha - Red-berried ones best ★★★

Guelder Rose - Smallish red berries in autumn ★★★ UK

Hawthorn – Tree with redish berries (haws) ★★ UK

Honeysuckle – Nice soft berries, not too large ★★★★ UK 🍃

Holly - Bright red berries late into winter ★★★ UK 🍃

Ivy – Small, black fruits just when needed ★★★★★ 🍃

Oregon grape - *Yellow bloom* with purple berries ★★★

Spindle Tree - Known as 'robin's bread' ★★★★★ UK 🍃

Wild Cherry - A small deciduous shrub or tree ★★★★ UK

🍃 = Evergeen   UK = Native to Britain

Robin's berry and fruit-planting wishlist

Anything from a humble holly bush to a fancy Oregon grape, there are, as you can see, all kinds of goodies for us robins that you can cultivate outside. You don't have to transform your entire garden of course, but our list will provide a few pointers to help you with establishing your very own bird-friendly haven in at least a part of it. The five-star ratings indicate certain types of plants, shrubs or trees that we really, *really* enjoy feeding from and which are also sometimes useful throughout the course of the year for other necessities like nesting, or roosting in safely at night: so real robin favourites. Others with just two or three stars, not so much, but we will take them if desperate.

And it's funny how the appetite changes when you get really, *really* hungry? When the ground is frozen and a robin like me finds himself chest-deep in the snow, *anything* will do then. Even the remains of a rotten old crabapple is preferable to going without or – worse – starving. I do hope it won't come to that this year, otherwise all those migrant robins that went away will definitely have the last laugh.

Finally, don't forget: most of the items included in our list are strictly for the birds – NOT for human consumption. Never nibble at fruits or berries in the wild unless you are certain they are not toxic to humans.

So now you have decided to improve your garden for the welfare of robins, there is just one more thing you need to take note of before rushing out to grab your shovel: local conditions.

Soil and climate

As all active gardeners will tell you, even when considering good old hardy British or European plants, not everything will be in harmony with your local soil and climate. Some plants for instance enjoy lots of sun. Some prefer shade. Certain plants won't grow well in chalky soil; other plants might prefer life in a peaty soil, and so on. There are no two gardens in this world that are totally alike, so don't shy away from doing a bit of spade work first, so to speak, to see what suits. Staff at your local garden centre will be able to advise you on what will work best for your type of soil or aspect. Don't be afraid to ask.

In the meantime, whatever you do, aim for plenty of variety, and remember: a diversity of suitable native plants will encourage more species of invertebrates. And that's just dandy for us robins too.

Folklore

There are thought to be an abundance of berries ahead of a bad winter when food supplies might be scarce. At least that's what folks say: that you can foretell the severity or otherwise of the coming season by examining the quantity of berries that appear on bushes and trees in the autumn. Country people have observed this correlation for centuries. That's useful, isn't it? And very convenient for us birds too, if you come to think about it, with the promise of providing just that little bit extra to tide us over if the winter weather turns really nasty.

However, lots of clever people have looked into this sort of thing and will tell you that it's just what's called 'folklore' and that there's no scientific truth behind it whatsoever. Well, who would have thought it? You could have knocked me down with a feather when I first heard that. And in fairness I suppose there is no logical reason why a bush should be concerned about helping birds, unless it's because we do also assist them in a funny sort of way by spreading their berries and seeds, which we pass through our gut and deposit in all sorts of distant places, enabling a new generation of bushes to take root. In other words, the bushes wouldn't want us all to die of hunger would they? It's what's called a symbiotic relationship – when one species helps out another.

The trouble is, I still can't figure out how a bush can forecast the weather. If that's true, then those clever people will need to sharpen their pencils and do quite a bit of re-calculating about the way things work in nature to make sense of *that*.

Anyway, I'm not going to trouble myself over mysteries. I'm far too busy eating. Some of these fruits are so succulent and delicious that even when I'm not all that hungry I just can't resist.

Robin with autumn berries

No, I'm not fat in that picture. How dare you! Some of those elder branches are very bendy at this time of the year, that's all.

Gardeners at work

Did you know that Robins have a particularly strong work ethic? It's true. And we're never happier than watching other people doing it. For example, we especially like to keep an eye on gardeners right now since they do say there is always so much to be getting on with – what with pruning and transplanting and clearing up outdoors after all those summer fun and games. This is when we like to follow you about most of all. Robins are great opportunists, and when we notice you chopping things down and digging things up, we know this means there will be lots of easy pickings and loads of little bugs and worms in the offing as we hop around behind you. Commensal feeding, as it's called.

These are the times when you'll also notice us becoming especially daring and cheeky, perched on your garden fork or singing loudly in the trees above your head just when you're concentrating and trying to remember something important you have to be doing.

The origin to all this goes back to olden times when robins in the wild woods would follow in the wake of much bigger creatures, like foxes, badgers or wild boar – the ancestors of your modern farmyard pigs. The boar would disturb the ground with their snouts or hooves, and we would just tag along and clear up anything that was left behind. So, even though it's not a very flattering comparison, gardeners for us are just like wild pigs. Sorry. That's very unkind of me, I know. But I am if nothing else an honest robin.

Not so tidy please, if you don't mind

Now I can perfectly understand why a lot of you horticultural types are fond of neatness; of tidy borders and well-ordered flower beds. Jolly good. Nothing wrong with that. But a garden that is *excessively* tidy can prove a bit of a let-down for your average robin. What I mean to say is please don't over do it! Try to resist the urge towards perfection and don't be in such a hurry to go clearing away all that old summer growth – at least not just yet.

Yes, I know, when you look outside or go for a stroll through the garden it might appear to be all horribly droopy and unkempt to you – all that old wood and rotting fruit – but to a bird this is breakfast, lunch and dinner in hard times. And if you cut down and clear up all over the place, so many of the lovely berries and seedheads that we rely on will vanish as well, and then there will be nothing left for us to forage for during the harsher times of the year.

Also, if you've got the space, you really can cultivate in yourself a genuine fondness for areas with mature plants. Old seedheads and twigs really can look fine, don't you think, when covered in little diamond dew droplets of a morning, or in the hoarfrost, and even in the snow? Yes, of course they do! In any case, I have it on good authority that lots of arty people reckon that old flower heads and bare shrubbery look beautiful as they mature and reach old age. 'There's an attractive aesthetic in the patina and noble architecture of mature plants', they say.

See!

Well, I don't know about all that. But robins certainly are very fond of anything that provides the goods – especially when we're feeling peckish, which actually tends to be the case more often than not. And old plants are just great for providing sustenance and shelter. In other words please cherish them too. Leave at least some of them right through to the end of winter if you can, and your resident robin will be full of praise.

First do no harm

Helping robins by cultivating the most suitable plants to see us through the tough old seasons of autumn and winter is a worthy consideration. But this is really only half the picture. For gardeners, it's not just about taking positive steps and being proactive in your care for wildlife. Sometimes gardeners also need to make sure they are not doing harm – that is occupying themselves with things that are actually hazardous to the welfare of birds.

For example, some notable absentees from the above list include berry-rich cotoneaster and Virginia creeper. Folks might well tell you these are great for birds – and indeed they can be. But these days both are considered to be 'invasive' varieties – plants from overseas that, once let loose, sometimes just don't know when to stop growing or proliferating. Consequently, they take up room and limit the natural diversity of native species that birds and other wildlife might already be relying on. I've even heard rumours that some garden centres sell plant varieties whose decorative berries have been modified to discourage birds from eating them. Disgraceful!

But it's not just about wrong planting. That's really the least of our worries. The array of chemicals in your typical gardener's shed can prove harmful to wildlife and especially insects when applied incorrectly. I can appreciate that you might not be all that fond of insects – but don't forget, birds eat them, and often rely on them for feeding their young. In other words, please be careful. Consider cultivating a kind of gardeners' Hippocratic oath: "First do no harm". This is a laudable sentiment, because it's easy to assume pest-controls or weed-killers are perfectly harmless when in reality they might not be at all safe for wildlife when used incorrectly or without due care.

Here, then, are some valuable tips on what not to be doing, and for which you could perhaps find alternatives that are safer for your local birds – minor alterations to your routine that can also make a big difference to the welfare and survival of all the living things in your garden, and which might even be beneficial to you and your family in the long run. First up ... the lawn.

Lawn care and maintenance

Now, if there's one thing in a garden that robins simply adore it's a nice well-mown lawn. And though it's no doubt true that for many folks the maintenance of a lawn is regarded as a bit of a chore, it is still infinitely preferable from a robin's point of view to the existence of vast swaths of concrete paving or wooden decking. This is because these things are sterile and without much life in them at all, whereas a lawn will invariably be a rich source of the staple diet of birds, namely earthworms. This is especially the case in wet weather when the worms venture up onto the surface. Not so much in the hot dry weather when they will have burrowed deep underground – but no matter; in those conditions the worms are usually replaced by lots of flies and other tiny invertebrates. And that's a fair exchange, I reckon.

Regarding maintenance, we prefer the grass to be kept short, if that's all right with you. Otherwise it's a nightmare when it comes to foraging and we have to negotiate all those irritating stems and bits of straw sticking up at just the height of a robin's eyes. Horrid. Long grass also prevents us seeing what's going on around us, which can be dangerous. So please keep it mown. And if you want to be really reckless, why not give it a soaking every once in a while with a sprinkler or hose during hot weather? As a gesture, it might not make a huge difference to the health of your lawn during a really hot, dry spell, but if you water in the evening the moisture won't evaporate so quickly and there might be at least a few juicy worms on the surface next morning for our breakfast.

So far so good, but a note of caution needs to be sounded even here because for all its bounty and joys that lawn of yours can also sometimes prove to be a mixed blessing. Yes, who would have thought it – that a nice innocent-looking green lawn might prove a danger to birds? But it can, *sometimes* – which brings me back to a very important subject indeed.

Chemical hazards

Unless absolutely necessary please try to refrain from using too many artificial substances to kill weeds or garden pests. Doing so can be dangerous for us robins.

Yes, I know it's tempting to resort to chemical treatments, especially for all those fine-leafed invasive weeds that are almost impossible to pick out by hand. You might be forced to go for something a little more potent then, but try keeping it to a minimum if you possibly can and always follow the instructions on the label.

It shouldn't come as a surprise, but the manufacturers of garden chemicals really aren't reckless or particularly wicked. They are aware of wildlife too, and they do want you to use their products responsibly – that is by applying the minimum quantities to get the job done. Don't be tempted to ignore the instructions on the label, to mix it stronger or to pour in a bit extra 'just to make sure'. Putting in *one for the pot* is a sound principal for making a nice cup of tea for the family, but not for applying stuff that could be lethal to wildlife.

Think about it for a moment. Supposing I come along and eat a worm or a beetle that has been paddling about in weed killer or fungicide. What do you imagine that does to my delicate little insides? It's probably not entirely great for you by the way. Not that you will be eating worms or beetles, but you might well be spreading these substances on your hands and clothes. Anything that harms the biology of any living thing will not do you any favours either, especially if you don't wear the proper protective gear. And of course the same concerns also apply to the welfare of your family and pets.

The remedy to all this is just to get on down and prick out as many of the bigger weeds as you can by hand. Doing things that way really doesn't take that much longer – not if you compare it to all the trouble of going off to the shops to buy weed killer, mixing it up, applying it and then cleaning up afterwards – not to mention all the time wasted when you forget where you stored the packet last year and then spend ages trying to locate it again in the garden shed. (Yes, I've seen you! Robins are very observant and we find it hilarious sometimes.)

The wonders of mulch

For dealing with smaller weeds in the flower and vegetable beds meanwhile, the very best thing in the world for keeping them in check is mulching. Mulch is a substance similar to soil but composed of well-rotted organic matter or leaf mould. The weed seeds won't germinate under a good layer of mulch where there's no light, and it's an easy substance to produce too. Make up a compost heap in a corner of your garden. Put all your garden waste and lawn trimmings into that and like magic it will break down within a few months to a delightful organic and – above all – *safe* substance that can be spread on the ground. Use plenty of it around your plants and vegetables.

Robins, too, adore mulch. In fact you could say that for us *you can never have too much mulch*. We can grub about in it and uncover multitudes of little bugs and creepy crawlies. And that's helpful to you too, because a healthy population of birds nibbling away in your garden really is the ultimate in pest control as we consume so many of the little nuisances that harm your plants – like all those greedy caterpillars and leatherjackets I mentioned earlier. If in doubt, just look again at those robin menus.

Yes, chemicals are helpful sometimes in extreme circumstances. And some are arguably far safer than others anyway. But the rule of thumb for a harmonious garden environment is simple: be as organic as possible, and you'll see the diversity of wildlife around you flourish like never before.

Out buildings – the perils lurking

Continuing on the subject of safety, robins have happily coexisted with people for centuries. And we've become quite partial to investigating all those peculiar stand-alone buildings that you put up but don't actually occupy yourselves, like sheds, garages, barns and so on. You might not always be aware or notice us using them, but – as you have seen throughout this book – we do sometimes make our nests there, or even roost inside occasionally. We are creatures of habit, so please make sure our ways in and out are not suddenly filled in or obstructed.

Garages, meanwhile, can throw up additional hazards because small birds are particularly prone to carbon monoxide poisoning. Car fumes can carry us off if we are exposed to idling engines in a confined space. Also, do take a care with those mousetraps please! Robins can easily end their days caught in them, especially if there is a nice tempting piece of cheese on view at the time. *Snap*, and we're done for. Please keep them somewhere concealed where we cannot get to them – like inside a box or piece of old piping. The mice can wriggle inside if they want to, but we won't bother if the entrance is too tiny.

Recalling the Robin's Year

As we reach the end of the robin's year, this is probably a good time to recap and summarise the whole story in one place.

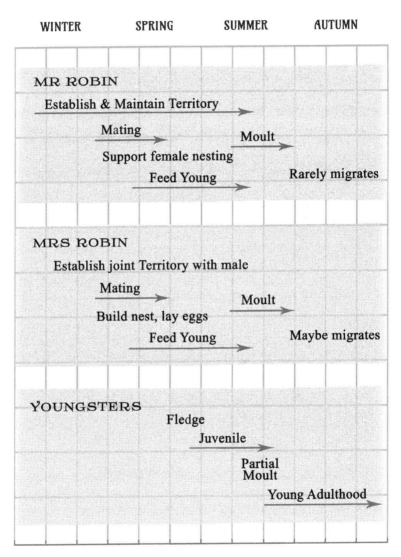

Summary of the year in the life of robins

On a very basic level we can view the typical robin year in terms of a four-fold structure, a seasonal division, with each one having its own distinctive tasks – winter being largely concerned with establishing territory, while spring is for mating and nesting. Summer is the time for recuperation and moulting, and autumn for migration (for some, anyway) while for those of us who remain at home it's a time to prepare for the lean spell of winter once more as the whole cycle begins to repeat itself. You can follow this in the accompanying calendar.

The main thing to bear in mind is that although a diagram of this kind makes for a pretty good rule of thumb, in practice any given year will present a complex and evolving picture, with lots of variables. So the dates indicated are by necessity approximate – like nesting, for example. Sometimes the first brood of chicks will come along much earlier than indicated, sometimes later. Occasionally, there will be a third brood that extends the nesting season beyond what is suggested. The migration times are also far from fixed. It varies.

And also, as we have seen, most of us robins here in the UK do not migrate at all. Some only wander off a few miles or less for a spell away from their former territory. Often they will return ahead of those who have migrated overseas, sometimes behind. It all depends on the weather, the food supply and how things look from a robin's perspective. Judgement is key – though sadly not always infallible.

For instance, and as I indicated earlier, if a female robin who has migrated overseas decides to return too soon, she might encounter a far more challenging end to our

British winter than she had anticipated and consequently a dangerous shortage of food at just the time when she needs it the most. If she comes back too late, on the other hand, she might discover that everything is already in full swing, and all the most virile and healthy male robins are already paired up with females. She will either have to settle for second best then or else be left on the shelf.

All these calculations need to be made in an intuitive sense. There are many unknowns that are simply beyond our control. If we don't manage to time things right, the repercussions can prove very unsettling or even fatal. That is why robin populations are seen to rise and fall so dramatically from year to year. A severe winter can result in a substantial reduction in our numbers, with only the strongest or smartest individuals surviving.

I suppose, also, when you consider how hard it is to find nourishment during the really difficult winter months, and of all the many different creatures out here who, hungry or even starving themselves, are aiming to eat robins, it's little short of a miracle that even a few of us get through such a tricky time. And in that respect you never quite know what's waiting around the corner.

The season's turning

So this book is finishing here at the very end of autumn. It's all change now, and not exactly for the best I regret to say because the air is already frosty and cold and there's a harshness to the garden landscape that seems to us older robins more bleak and unforgiving than ever. It's worse somehow, because all the friendly voices of the people we have come to know and recognise have already fallen silent and retreated inside – much earlier it seems this year – and really anything could happen to a robin out here in the wild on its own.

I'm not sure if I like winter any more. And I wish it would not come. Not only is it more difficult to find anything to eat but the nights become so much longer than in summer, so it seems like an endlessly cold wait in the darkness before any opportunity for breakfast comes around the next day – even if you can find it!

And although a whole year is an enormously long period in the life of a robin, experience tells me it must be that time again when the leaves on the trees dry up and you hear that crisp rustle when the wind blows across them for the final time before they fall to the ground. Then there's suddenly not so much cover for me to hide in if I become frightened. Because even brave robins can feel a little frightened sometimes. Did you know that?

Robin with falling oak leaves

Yes, you really can fall into thinking about all kinds of strange and sombre things at a time like this. There really is something terribly threatening about things – all those angry gales and storms that come along so unexpectedly, and those towering clouds (wherever do they end?) and the trees in the woods beneath them that remind me of the arches of some ruined old building – so eerie and full of echoes when the winds fall silent.

And then nearer the ground where I live and feed there's all the fallen bracken and the slippery leaves and bare branches on every bush and stem that all seem so hard and brittle and unforgiving, that you sometimes feel you are hopping along through the gnarled old fingers of a host of witches just waiting to reach out and grab you.

Oh dear! I'd better not dwell on all this too much. I mustn't let myself become morbid. Even though they say the average life expectancy of your typical garden robin is only a year or so, that's just because most of us perish in the first few months of life – usually by not being able to fend for ourselves or by being taken by predators. Some lucky robins live on for years once they get past those first few difficult months.

Perhaps I shall be like that.

I once heard a story about a gardener who told a robin that if conditions ever turned really bad his door would always be open and that the robin would be welcome if he just wanted to hop in, and that there he would be loved and looked after. Well ... that seemed a bit much for the robin. We are after all only creatures of the wild.

And you'd have to have a lot of faith to do a thing like that, wouldn't you?

I'll be OK. Don't worry. I'll get through. And I'll probably see you again on the other side of winter, eh? When the days lengthen and spring and warmth return to the earth.

Only I wouldn't entirely rely on it, *if I were you.*

GLOSSARY

Anting – the curious actions of a robin when it picks up an ant in its beak and appears to trail it through its feathers. A small quantity of formic acid released by the distressed ant acts against parasites in the robin's plumage.

Bigamy – the scandalous behaviour of a robin already in a partnership when it forms a third–party relationship with another robin. Robins of both sexes are prone occasionally to bigamous behaviour.

Bill – the term some people like to use for our beaks (thus, if your pet canary is named Bill, his beak would be called Bill's bill).

Brood – a collective term for the number of young successfully hatched within a nest.

Brooding – the spreading of wings gently upon the eggs or nestlings to protect them and keep them warm and dry, particularly during the early days after hatching.

Brood patch – an area on the abdomen of a female robin that is void of feathers during the nesting season, enabling her body heat to conduct more effectively onto the surface of her eggs. The patch disappears and is replaced by regular plumage after nesting is over.

Cloaca *(Plural = cloacae)* – an anatomical term that refers to the internal cavity from which the urinary and intestinal organs of birds have their opening, and within which the sexual organs are also operative. Copulation occurs when the cloacae of the male and female robins come briefly into contact.

Clutch – the total number of eggs laid in the nest by a female robin. Typically between 4 and 6 eggs, though 7 is not uncommon, and in rare instances even more have been recorded.

Cock – the proper term for a male robin, but not used in this book.

Commensal feeding – a term applied when birds supplement their diets by following other creatures about, like gardeners, who stir up invertebrates and other prey as they go about their work.

Copulation – the act of sexual intercourse between creatures. This only occurs during a few months in the year for robins, but we do try to make the most of it.

Dehydration – the process in which an organism becomes stressed from losing more fluid than it takes in. Adequate levels of water are essential for numerous vital biological functions. Thirst is a sign of being dehydrated.

Erithacus the scientific name for the robin species – the magnificent English robin, the subject of this book, being of the sub-species Erithacus Rubecula.

Fledge – a verb describing the process during which a young bird gains a full compliment of feathers, enabling it to leave the nest and fly. *To fledge.*

Fledgling – a young robin who has just vacated its nest and flown (after a fashion) for the first time. The term is only applied for the first few days. Thereafter, the term 'juvenile' is used to describe a young robin.

Hatchling – the very young robin just after it has hatched – that is, having broken through the shell of its egg and emerged.

Hen – the proper term for a female robin – a Mrs Robin, that is – and certainly not used in these pages.

Hydration – a term describing the essential process by which a living organism, a person or a bird for instance, absorb water or other fluids – normally through drinking.

Incubation – the process of sitting on eggs by the female robin in order to convey her body heat to them. The warmth encourages the embryo inside to begin growing and eventually to hatch from its shell.

Invertebrates – creatures who do not have a backbone or skeletal system. Insects and spiders are invertebrates and robins are very fond of them. Instead of bones, they tend to have a slightly hardened outer casing to provide structure and protection. Pleasantly crunchy.

Juvenile – the young robin who has established his flight feathers – a stage reached a few days after leaving the nest. The term continues to be applied right up until the time of its partial moult in late summer when its adult plumage and red-breast feathers finally emerge.

Migration – the process of travelling over long distances during the winter months to more pleasant climes – the journey being reversed a few months later when a robin returns home in time for the new breeding season.

Nestling – a popular term applied to a young robin developing and growing its feathers within the confines of the nest.

Moult – the annual loss of feathers followed by their eventual replacement with new ones. For adult robins this occurs during the late summer period, after nesting and rearing of the young is over and can take several long and difficult weeks.

Mulching – the process of applying well-rotten compost or leaf mould to the soil. It keeps weeds at bay and provides a rich source of nutrition for birds.

Preening – the act of aligning feathers with the beak, and during which oil from the uropygial gland is trailed through the plumage.

Roost – the place where birds go at night to sleep. Roosting or 'going to roost' = the act of finding a suitable sleeping place.

Symbiotic Relationship - an interdependent or partially interdependent relationship between species featuring some aspect of shared or mutual benefit.

Uropygial Gland – the small gland situated on a robin's lower back near the base of its tail and from which an oily substance can be extracted to assist in the preening of feathers. The oil also acts as a water repellent.

.

Editor's Note

Just a quick word concerning the title of this book and the peculiar idea, as suggested on the cover, that the author (A. Robin, Esq) set about writing it after perhaps discovering an old typewriter hidden in the undergrowth. Obviously this is not true, and someone would really have to be pretty naïve if not downright *weird* to imagine such an undertaking could be even remotely plausible. For a start, how could a robin or indeed any species of bird manage to load the necessary sheets of paper into such a machine? How could it operate the old-style manual carriage return each time the end of a line was reached? It's nonsense of course, and I would just like to take this opportunity to assure readers that nobody involved in the production of this book is urging you to accept what is clearly an irrational fantasy. The truth is he did the whole thing on a laptop.

I hope this clears up any misconceptions.

The author

'Hark at that little fellow up there! Is that not how a man should be? Our feathered friend here has but a short time on this Earth, oppressed by dangers and hardships on every side, and yet he puffs out his chest and shows off and sings his heart out until he dies. A fine philosophy.'

From the novel 'Wildish' by Robert Stephen Parry

INDEX

The Index begins by providing some quick-fire answers to frequently-asked questions.

Traditional Index

A

B

C

D

L

Legs 11-12
Lice 133-134, 136

Lifespan 9
Logpile 67-69

M

Magpies 77-78, 110-111
Mating season 22-23, 55-56
Mealworms 21
Migration 132, 155-159

Moult 65, 137-144
Mousetraps 188
Mulching 186-187

N

Names 40-42
Nesting box 73-81
Nest construction 72-73

Nest Hygiene 93-94
Nest location 68-71, 77-78
Nest occupancy 97-98

O

Out-building hazards 187

Opportunists 180

P

Pairing up 22-23, 55-57
Plumage 42-43, 96, 109
Preening 32-33

Predators 78-79, 109-115
Primaries 137-138
Protection of nests 66-68, 79

R

Robins Bread 174-175
Redbreast name 40-42
Red breast 28, 42, 137, 144,
Rodents 111, 113

Ruddock 41-42
Roosting 12, 166, 190
Robinet 41

S

Secondaries 138-139
Sex differentiation 47, 65-66
Sight 129
Singing 22, 25-26, 60, 106,
160-162
Size 8

Snakes 78, 111, 113
Song 22, 60, 106, 107,
Squirrels 66, 111
Sparrowhawk 111-112
Spiders 17, 86-87, 152
Spindle tree 174-175

POSTSCRIPT

Cor ... look at this: it's spring – and I'm still here! Even though I finished this book a long time ago, I thought I should just pop back and peck out a few more lines to let you know that I'm alive and well, that Mrs Robin has returned and the days are lengthening, it's getting warm, and that all the trees are full of leaf and blossom and everywhere is a big, big adventure once again.

Anyway, I hope you enjoyed learning all about me and the other robins. It's a nice little book, isn't it? Send a copy or two to your friends – because it makes a great Christmas present. And don't forget: whatever the problems, whatever the adversities or dangers you're going through right now, life is good – or as us robins always say, 'Keep your pecker up'.

Printed in Poland
by Amazon Fulfillment
Poland Sp. z o.o., Wrocław
12 June 2022

e6d62391-2e6f-44cf-b5da-04e9681b32edR01